GETTING
THE BALANCE
RIGHT

GETTING THE BALANCE RIGHT

LEADING AND MANAGING WELL

PETER SHAW

Marshall Cavendish
Business

Copyright © 2013 Peter Shaw
Cover design: Cover Kitchen Co. Limited

Published in 2013 by Marshall Cavendish Business
An imprint of Marshall Cavendish International
1 New Industrial Road, Singapore 536196
genrefsales@sg.marshallcavendish.com
www.marshallcavendish.com/genref

Other Marshall Cavendish offices:
Marshall Cavendish Corporation. 99 White Plains Road, Tarrytown NY 10591-
9001, USA • Marshall Cavendish International (Thailand) Co Ltd. 253 Asoke,
12th Flr, Sukhumvit 21 Road, Klongtoey Nua, Wattana, Bangkok 10110,
Thailand • Marshall Cavendish (Malaysia) Sdn Bhd. Times Subang, Lot 46,
Subang Hi-Tech Industrial Park, Batu Tiga, 40000 Shah Alam, Selangor Darul
Ehsan, Malaysia

Marshall Cavendish is a trademark of Times Publishing Limited

The right of Peter Shaw to be identified as the author of this work has been
asserted by him in accordance with the Copyright, Designs and Patents Act
1988.

ISBN 978-981-4328-31-9

Printed and bound in Great Britain by
TJ International Limited, Padstow, Cornwall

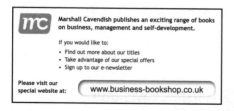

Dedicated to Anna, Owen and Holly, who have each brought energy and thoughtfulness into our family life and bring a delightful sense of fun.

CONTENTS

FOREWORD

Getting the balance right is never easy. This book will provide you with valuable insights and practical ideas.

The questions the book addresses are highly relevant in a demanding and fast-changing world. When do you lead and when do you follow? When are principles key and when is a pragmatic approach more important? How can you be engaged and detached at the same time? How best do you keep your rational and emotional responses in tune with each other? How do you build a virtuous circle of being responsive and directive? How do you balance ambition and acceptance? How can you be both serious and joyful?

All these questions resonate strongly with me. With leadership responsibility for 50,000 people in Accenture across a third of the world, I am acutely aware of my own need to balance the considerations covered in this book. Much of the mentoring I do of senior leaders is about enabling them to find the right balance and equilibrium on these key axes.

Peter brings a wealth of experience as a former director general in the UK Government, an executive coach of teams and individuals across five continents and as a business school professor. Peter writes in an engaging and practical way with no jargon. Each of the short chapters provides valuable prompts for thought and action.

This is a book that could radically change your approach to leading and managing. It will enable you to stand back and reflect. It will help you understand better your reactions in different situations. It will enable you to crystallize your approach in handling demanding issues in the future, both as an individual and as part of a team. The book is equally relevant whatever country you live in or sector you work in.

Be ready for your thinking, attitudes and approaches to change as you read this book.

Jeremy Oates
Managing Director of Technology for Europe,
Africa, Middle East and Latin America
Accenture

INTRODUCTION

I get enormous pleasure from doing long-distance walks. As a walker you have to achieve a balance. The right balance will vary depending on the weight of the load you are carrying: whether the terrain is rocky, smooth or boggy; the nature of the gradient; and whether you are feeling fit or tired. The length of stride and the pace will vary depending on the time of day, whether you are walking alone or in a group, and how the mood of the day takes you.

Our journey through life is not dissimilar. On some days we feel energised and able to address any challenge. On other occasions we feel daunted and the shallowest, upward gradient seems like a long drudge. There is no magic formula for getting the balance right. We learn to be adaptable to the environment around us, the expectations of others, the pressures we feel under and our own moods.

The long distance walker knows that the best way to keep their balance is to look forward and be clear about the direction they are travelling, both half a mile ahead and five steps ahead. The walker is infinitely adaptable, holding on to a rock while going around big boulders, using a walking pole on rough ground, or treading carefully through boggy marshland. The walker enjoys the variety, relishes the company of others, celebrates reaching their destination and appreciates that every walk is different.

Getting the balance right in our work, and in the relationship between work and the rest of life, is not about applying a fixed, rigid formula. Success comes through understanding yourself as clearly as possible, understanding the politics and emotions of the environment around you, and holding your nerve when visibility is diminished and you are feeling damp and soggy.

I explore 12 areas where getting the balance right is crucial in order to lead and manage well, for both your well-being and your success. These 12 areas provide prompts for thought and a stimulus for action:

- following and leading
- engagement and detachment
- principle and pragmatism
- awareness and action
- rational and emotional
- individual and collective
- directive and responsive
- realism and optimism
- continuity and change
- present and future
- ambition and acceptance
- serious and joyful

Under each section I explore four different aspects using examples, setting out practical ideas and points for reflection.

I offer no magic formula. My intention is to set out practical ideas to enable the reader to reach their own conclusions about what is the right point of balance. There are always choices to be made, even if it is only regarding our attitude. The long-distance walker keeps making choices about the direction they are travelling and where they are going to put their feet next. They are continually choosing their point of balance, sometimes deliberately and sometimes instinctively. If this book stimulates you to see your choices in new ways, then it is serving the purpose for which it was intended.

Long-distance walks may not be your particular pleasure, but seeing how you adapt your balance when walking, running, cycling, skiing or swimming can provide a practical illustration of the need for strength and adaptability in getting the balance right.

The book does not separately address the balance between work and the rest of life. I sought to do that in *Thriving in Your Work* (Marshall Cavendish, 2011) and *Raise Your Game* (Capstone, 2009). The points of balance covered in this book address the whole of life and are just as relevant whether you are in paid employment, working in a voluntary capacity, or have full-time family or caring responsibilities.

Enjoy the reflections in this book and when your balance fails you and you fall over, dust yourself off, consider what you have learnt, laugh and move on.

Peter Shaw
Godalming, England
peter.shaw@praesta.com

FOLLOWING AND LEADING

The choir whose music inspires us will have one conductor and an alert and well-rehearsed group of choral singers. The conductor signals to the choir that they are about to begin and holds the baton ready. The conductor holds the moment prior to signalling that the first note is to be sung. The conductor moves the baton and the choir comes in as with one voice...

For the choir to be successful there has to be one leader and many followers. Both need to play their part well or the choir will sing poorly. If the choral singers are unconvinced about the conductor, they will move to another choir or vote out the conductor at the annual meeting. If the conductor is not impressed with the choral singers, he or she is likely to move elsewhere. So the balance between leading and following in a choir is tested with every performance.

This section looks at different aspects of following and leading, namely: who do you follow; what does leading mean; can you follow and lead at the same time; and why should anyone follow you?

Chapter 1

WHO DO YOU FOLLOW?

When a new government has been appointed, as a civil servant, it is your responsibility to respond constructively to the newly-elected political leadership. When a new chief executive has been appointed in a commercial organisation it is your responsibility as an employee to respond constructively to the leadership of the new chief executive. In both cases the employee is paid either by the taxpayer or by the revenue of the commercial organisation to do a particular job.

Some people will follow with more energy and commitment than others. Some leaders get our support because we take pride in doing a job well. Other leaders will get much more from us because they inspire and motivate us to go beyond the normal daily expectations.

If we follow because we regard it as our duty to do so, we will make progress in a dogged sort of way. But if we follow because we are inspired and motivated, our progress is likely to be much more engaged, buoyant and joyful.

We normally follow people who catch our imagination, and whose words and deeds lift our spirits. They need to be convincing and know what they are talking about. We need to feel we can trust them and their judgement. The leader who inspires creates a desire in us to push the boundaries and make progress, which can contrast with others who have not brought out the best in us.

Natalie loved working for Helen and felt Helen was a superb role model. Helen had worked hard to build the reputation of the team. She understood what the chief executive wanted and interpreted that clearly to her staff. Helen had built good links with her peers in the organisation and knew how to influence and persuade. Helen was able to forewarn Natalie when difficult issues were about to arise. Natalie felt both protected and challenged by Helen, who was a good mentor to her.

Natalie reflected on why Helen brought out the best in her. It was because Helen led by doing what only she could do, which was about upwards management and steering the work of the team. Helen created space for Natalie to do her job well. Helen brought a wider perspective, which gave Natalie the context for her work. Natalie could always approach Helen to talk through tricky issues. In most cases Helen left the final decision to Natalie, who felt motivated and energised. Natalie's confidence and competence kept growing because she was following a leader who gave her space to grow.

Following is not just about following your boss. It can be about following the example of a range of different people both inside and outside the organisation in which you work. Sometimes it might be following the example of someone more junior in the organisation who brings an approach to the work that you particularly admire. Developing the skill of following might be about identifying a range of people whose approaches and values you respect and want to learn from.

Being a good follower might mean grabbing someone's attention and asking them why they handled a particular situation in a certain way. How would you bring out the best from people in difficult circumstances, or from someone who has inspired you on your journey? The good follower soaks up learning from lots of different people and then crystallizes that learning down to two or three points that are relevant for them.

Being a good follower does not mean allowing ourselves to be pulled in many different directions at the same time. It is about being clear of our responsibilities, clear in distilling our learning, selective in our choice of role models while recognising both our strengths and imperfections. Good following is never about embracing an approach in its entirety. It is about choosing carefully which aspects you want to embrace. Following heroes blindly is not what good following is about!

WHO DO YOU FOLLOW?

- To whom are you responsible and are your accountabilities clear to them?
- Who do you believe you can learn a lot from?
- Who has had similar experiences to you whose insights might be relevant for you?
- When might there be a risk of hero worship and how do you ensure that you avoid blind belief?
- How best are you selective in deciding which aspects of someone you follow?
- How best do you balance allowing yourself to be inspired by someone, while keeping objectivity about the merits of their approach?
- When do you need to be more sceptical about who you are following?

POINTS FOR REFLECTION

- How discriminating are you in the way you follow those to whom you are responsible?
- Whose ideas and approaches do you want to learn from and follow?
- Who might you want to follow with either less enthusiasm or more commitment?

Chapter 2

WHAT DOES LEADING MEAN?

The drill sergeant leads their squad by shouting out precise instructions. If their orders are not obeyed to the letter the squad sergeant rebukes the soldiers with a directness that might make the onlooker squirm. The ship's captain leads a ship's crew both by giving clear instructions and by ensuring that each junior officer leads his or her part of the crew well. For the ship's captain leading is both about accountability for safety and getting to the destination on time, alongside setting clear expectations for their staff and motivating them to fulfil their responsibilities well.

Leading has an element of telling, but the good leader builds shared endeavour – inspiring, engaging and motivating. The good leader's influence spreads throughout an organisation as people mirror the standards and approaches set by the leader.

When working with senior management teams I will often ask them how they would like to be described by their people. One team recently listed the words that they would like their staff to use about them: in touch, engaged, effective, powerful, influential, purposeful, practical, authoritative and collaborative. My encouragement to them was to be clear which of these descriptors was most important and then to think hard about the conditions that would need to be in place before people would use those descriptors. Having described the necessary conditions, I encouraged the team members to be committed to work in such a way that the evidence is readily available. For example: if they want to be described as engaged, there would need to be lots of evidence that they are engaged with different interest groups and staff right across the organisation.

Jeremy wanted to become a good leader of his department. He had read lots of books on leadership and been on a variety of courses. His mind was full of a mish-mash of principles and examples. Jeremy knew he had to be selective – if he imposed a model from elsewhere his staff would shrug their shoulders. Jeremy recognised that he needed to make time to listen. He needed to understand the context, the pressures people were under and the expectations of both stakeholders and staff.

Jeremy drew from his previous experience. He talked to a mentor who had led a similar type of organisation. He worked with a coach who had a wide experience of different types of organisations. Jeremy sought to distil the information he was picking up. He trusted his intuitive reactions and built a picture in his own mind about the strengths and weaknesses within the organisation and what needed to be done. He sounded out people he trusted about their perception and about some of his ideas for moving forward. Jeremy kept coming back to the outcomes that were expected. Leading was not about imposing a particular view. It was about building a sense of common purpose and endeavour to reach a set of outcomes that were understood and accepted.

Leading can be about enabling people to hold their nerve and about providing a safe space in which ideas can be developed and taken forward. It can involve ensuring that appropriate resources are available and that different types of experience and expertise can be tapped.

The small firm that Ben ran was going through a difficult patch. Ben knew he had to win some new customers while not looking as if he was panicking. He had to keep cool and calm in the way he ran his company. He needed to be realistic with his staff about the economic issues, while demonstrating the practical steps he was taking. They trusted in him and kept their anxiety under reasonable control, because they saw the measured attitude he adopted and the practical steps he was taking.

Leading is often about setting a tone. If the leader is measured and calm then others in the organisation are likely to take on a similar demeanour. If the leader is edgy, cross and impetuous, this will be regarded as the normal behaviour and will be followed by others.

WHAT DOES LEADING MEAN?

- Knowing when to tell and when to listen.
- Recognising the things only you can do.
- Bringing clarity to the context in which people are operating.
- Setting clear expectations.
- Adapting your approach to meet the needs of different individuals.
- Ensuring that there are always opportunities to clarify expectations.
- Understanding how people view your leadership.
- Ensuring there is enough evidence to underpin the leadership qualities and approach that you want to exemplify.
- Not taking yourself too seriously and being ready to laugh at your mistakes.

POINTS FOR REFLECTION

- Can you reflect on a difficult situation you are handling and the leadership approach you need to bring to help ensure an effective resolution?
- Over the next few weeks how are you going to get the balance right between telling, enabling and motivating?
- How do you want people to be describing you as a leader in three months' time?

Chapter 3

CAN YOU FOLLOW AND LEAD AT THE SAME TIME?

The leader of a publishing house leads the organisation through setting clear objectives, providing a disciplined structure, ensuring the financial management is robust and recruiting and developing the right people. But the leader of a publishing house also needs to create an understanding where individual editors can follow their interests within a changing context. The good commissioning editor needs to be both bold and cautious as they explore different markets and work with authors. The publishing house chief executive has got to trust their editors to find good commissions that will bring in decent revenues and build the reputation of the company.

In an IT software development company the managing director needs to nurture creativity. She has to inspire creative experts to devise new approaches to solving problems. She has to follow her instincts about what will work or not work.

Perhaps the good leader is always a follower. The thoughtful leader will have in their mind those leaders from their previous experience whose approaches they intuitively follow. They might also remember the principles or values which they regard as characteristics of good leadership and which they are seeking to embody in their own approach. One of my early books was entitled *Mirroring Jesus as a Leader* (Grove, 2004). This focused on six aspects of Jesus' leadership, namely: visionary, servant, teach, coach, radical and healer. The intention was to identify characteristics of a respected leader and then ask questions about the extent to which those six characteristics might be relevant for leaders today. The same type of approach could be applied to any highly respected leader.

The parent of a toddler will follow the child around as the youngster explores and experiments. The responsibility on the parent is about the safety of the toddler and the creation of a space where the youngster can learn. Good parenting is about giving toddlers freedom within boundaries and allowing toddlers to follow their interests and curiosity.

The parent of the teenager hopes that some of the disciplines and values of family life will have been embedded. In this phase of development parents have to lead by standing back and letting the teenager make their own mistakes. The boundaries need to be flexible as stern leadership by the parent is likely to be counter-productive.

The examples above of the parent as leader illustrate the difficult balance between leading and following in bringing out the best in others and allowing them to develop their creativity, stretch their own boundaries and learn from their mistakes.

Many successful leaders in the workplace regard it as crucial to be involved in activities outside the work environment where they are following and not leading. Barry is a senior executive in the oil industry who gets huge pleasure out of being an assistant coach for an under 11s football team. In one environment he has the responsibility to lead and direct. In another he is following the lead of the senior coach and helping boys develop footballing skills.

This contrast is important for Barry's personal equilibrium. Being a follower in one aspect of his life helps him appreciate both the responsibility and opportunity of being a leader at work. Being a follower helps Barry appreciate what motivates a follower and what the particular satisfactions are in being a contributor rather than taking the leading role.

HOW BEST DO YOU LEAD AND FOLLOW AT THE SAME TIME?

- Who do you observe leading and following effectively?
- When can the desire to follow get in the way of leading well?
- When can the sense of responsibility as a leader result in you trying too hard and not following enough?
- Who do you need to both follow and lead and how will you do that?
- How do you gauge the interests and curiosity of those you are leading?
- Across the whole of your life, what is the balance between leading and following and what would you like it to become?
- Might you do more activities where you follow in order to keep fresh your understanding of what is needed to lead well?

POINTS FOR REFLECTION

- If you are doing a lot of following at the moment, where might you take a lead?
- If you are doing a lot of leading at the moment, in what areas of your life might you do some following?
- In which situations might you consciously both follow and lead?

Chapter 4

WHY SHOULD ANYONE FOLLOW YOU?

The leader of any local voluntary organisation – be it an arts society, a walking club, a discussion group or a church – knows volunteers can be fickle. The commitment to participate must be heartfelt: but unless there is a desire to contribute on a regular basis, enthusiasm can wane. The membership of a voluntary organisation can dissipate quickly if the members or adherents do not really follow the leader.

For employees there is a financial dependency on the leader that does not exist in a voluntary organisation, but individuals will still make decisions to move when they have the opportunity. Similarly, the dictatorial head teacher is likely to lose their most creative staff over time.

A senior leadership team wanted to build a greater sense of shared endeavour with their staff. They talked about their role as a senior team and how they wanted to impact on the organisation. They summarised their role as shaping, modelling, engaging and galvanising. These words were important to them in illustrating how they wanted to behave. The stress on shaping was about steering and creating a framework rather than prescribing how things should be done. The emphasis on modelling was because the team was conscious that they were observed closely – they needed to demonstrate how they were working in partnership to encourage other people within the organisation to do the same.

The focus on engagement was about reinforcing the need to be actively listening to partners, customers and colleagues. The stress on galvanising was to legitimise the focus on energising and motivating those within the organisation. The team was clear that these four characteristics needed to be exemplified by the leadership team when they met as a group and also by them individually as leaders in their own areas.

"Why should anyone follow you?" is a powerful question for any individual or team to ask. It forces the questioner to recognise that individuals have choices. They may, in accountability terms, have to follow you, but only up to a point. They do not have to give you a high level of commitment.

People will follow you if they judge your aspirations and approach to be right. They may be applying key tests like:
- Is the leader credible?
- Are they setting out in a direction that is justifiable?
- Are they convincing in the way they describe the desired outcomes?
- When I hear them talk am I encouraged or dismayed?
- Are they generating a level of emotional commitment that takes me by surprise?
- Do they inspire me to make a contribution that is bigger than I might otherwise have given?

Addressing those types of questions honestly can help you prioritise the steps you want to take. Recognising both the rational and the emotional factors is necessary if you want a robust commitment from your staff.

Jeffrey was appointed as the manager of a football team that had recently had a sequence of poor results. The team was dejected and saw Jeffrey as one of a long line of managers who had stayed for a limited period. His arrival was not met with enthusiasm. Jeffrey's aim was to get to know each of the players well to understand both their skills and motivation. He spent time with them as individuals and observed them as a team. He let his deputy do most of the day-to-day coaching. Jeffrey wanted to observe when the players were motivated and when they were going through the motions.

Jeffrey saw his primary objective as presenting a clear set of aspirations for the team and persuading each of them that they could make a more significant contribution. He used his understanding of different personalities to decide which approach would work best with each player. Some needed gentle encouragement, while others needed a stiff talking to. The players responded to him well because Jeffrey understood them and knew how to motivate them as individuals and as a team.

WHY SHOULD ANYONE FOLLOW YOU?

- Can you identify which of your values and approaches particularly appeals to those who work with you?
- When are you at your best in inspiring others?
- When do you create partnerships most effectively?
- What feedback do you get from others about why they follow you?
- What support and thanks do you give to those who follow you?

POINTS FOR REFLECTION

- Who would you want to follow you, and what action might you take so they would decide to follow?
- How best do you build a stronger partnership with those who want to follow you?

ENGAGEMENT AND DETACHMENT

How can you be fully engaged and detached at the same time? Is this a desirable state or a realistic possibility? If you are fully engaged, has the prospect of objectivity disappeared? Does remaining completely detached mean you lose any sense of partnership, shared endeavour or ownership?

This section considers the balance between engagement and detachment by looking at taking engagement deeper, reflecting on when engagement can become manipulative, examining situations where either detachment or engagement has to take priority, and exploring how you can be engaged and detached at the same time.

Chapter 5
TAKING ENGAGEMENT DEEPER

Some people hanker after simple and clear lines of authority where requests are made and action taken. A view of the world where all engagement is transactional appears simple and straightforward, with no danger of misunderstanding as instructions are given and obeyed.

Successful engagement rarely has these straightforward characteristics. When engagement is purely transactional, the level of responsiveness and motivation is often low. The parent knows that on some occasions they can simply issue an instruction to their children and it will be followed. But effective engagement between parent and child is much deeper and more subtle than merely issuing instructions.

Effective engagement with staff can be forgotten in times of change and uncertainty. We can so easily convince ourselves that there is no time, or that engagement needs to wait until the picture is clearer. The reality is that effective engagement is even more important at these times.

Based on the experience of leaders and managers in a range of organisations, it is apparent that effective engagement involves relationships based on trust, effective listening, common purpose, shared endeavour and emotional self-awareness.

Creative debate within relationships based on trust is crucial, so that purposeful dialogue can release new ideas and not be a distraction. Inter-departmental battles, individual power struggles and blame cultures kill trust. Trust through engagement can never be taken for granted: it needs regular attention and investment of time, energy and emotion.

Building trust requires being genuinely committed to understanding where others are coming from and what success looks like for them. At the same time recognising who you can trust is important. Sometimes there is a limited basis for trust and all you can do is listen hard and try to have reasonable conversations that gradually take trust to a more secure level.

Central to building engagement is effective listening to those with an interest at any level, while not being sucked into narrow team or departmental perspectives. Success comes through bringing a quality of listening that is both "full on", discerning and discriminating. It requires giving your sole, undivided attention while seeing the wider picture at the same time.

Effective partnerships with good-quality engagement flow from building shared agendas and a sense of common purpose right across an organisation. Some colleagues may tend to build or reinforce barriers, particularly in periods of change. Partnerships where feedback can be given and received openly and sensitively are far more likely to survive, thrive and create shared success in times of change.

It is evident from a wide range of organisations that when individuals are dedicated to both shared goals and each other's success then the result is good quality engagement that leads to committed and flexible teams and groups. Teams that have limited professional and personal engagement will rarely provide the leadership necessary to grasp the future effectively.

The team that knows what each person brings and how and when its members engage effectively will have a measure of robustness that will enable it to keep its resolve in tough times. This may involve re-examining a team's purpose on a regular basis as the quality of engagement can decline when the operational impetus for a team becomes less significant.

The good team member will be emotionally self-aware, so that they bring an understanding of when their emotions are getting in the way and inhibiting effective engagement, be they feelings of apprehension, frustration, fear or tiredness.

Taking engagement deeper is not straightforward. It involves an investment of time and energy. It is not always simple, as overtures to build engagement may be rejected and you can feel rebuffed. But investing in engagement builds a stronger likelihood of motivation and long-term partnership. Time spent engaging with others is rarely wasted, while recognising that there will often be difficult decisions about priorities in the use of time and energy.

TAKING ENGAGEMENT DEEPER

- Build connections with others emotionally as well as intellectually.
- Take responsibility for raising the quality of engagement with your peers and your team.
- Encourage honesty and, when required, be challenging in engagement.
- Ensure engagement stands the test of time and of disagreements by building and re-establishing trust.
- Identify the protagonists whom you are least comfortable with and focus on effective engagement with them.
- Practice good quality engagement even when the wider organisation does not seem to support it.
- Recognise that the more you look outside yourself and mentor and encourage others, the greater will be your sense of fulfilment.

POINTS FOR REFLECTION

- With whom are you in danger of having a purely transactional relationship?
- With whom do you need to take engagement to a deeper level in order to ensure a greater sense of common purpose and shared endeavour?
- Where might trust be weak and a greater level of engagement built up?

Chapter 6

WHEN DOES ENGAGEMENT BECOME MANIPULATIVE?

Engagement can include asking questions, influencing, persuading and manipulating. When you observe a parent with a one year old, the parent will be using all these techniques. The approach might start with the question, "Are you ready for lunch?" but become "Now is the right time for lunch"; it might develop into "You must have your lunch or you will be hungry this afternoon", and might end up as "If you do not have your lunch there will be no chocolate after lunch".

From a young age we become used to our parents and others engaging with us through a sequence of questions – influencing, persuading and manipulating. As a youngster grows, asking questions becomes more likely to succeed as a technique, with subtle incentives inevitably playing a part. During the teenage years, attempts at manipulation can become much more explosive and counter-productive.

A teacher with energetic students can rely on questions as a means of keeping the pupils engaged and motivated. Curiosity and a sense of healthy competition can keep motivation high when good, open-ended questions are asked. But ultimate sanctions may still be needed if unwilling pupils are to be persuaded that their homework needs to be done!

The executive coach working with leaders and managers knows that the most effective engagement comes through the use of perceptive questions, so that the individual reaches their own conclusions about their own next steps. The coach who tries to influence or persuade loses their neutrality, is at risk of creating dependency and can become treated with suspicion rather than respect. A leader or manager is there to influence as well as to ask questions. They will have a role in persuading organisations and individuals about the merit of particular courses of action.

Where is the dividing line between persuasion and manipulation and why is it acceptable for a parent to sometimes manipulate a baby or toddler's behaviour and not acceptable for an adult to try to manipulate the behaviour of another adult? We are constantly bombarded with advertising that tries to persuade us to buy certain products. Often the emotional approach is overtly manipulative, and yet we enjoy being flattered and enticed. But as soon as we feel blatantly manipulated, we become disenchanted and our view of the product or service can rapidly diminish.

A good measure of whether you are manipulating others is to think how you would act if you were treated in a similar way. Manipulation is a dangerous game that can destroy trust and any sense of shared purpose. Speaking ill words behind someone's back is perhaps the most obvious example of manipulation that destroys trust and can erode the reputation of the gossiper far more than the subject of the comments.

You are in danger of manipulating when you deliberately tell only part of a story, use emotional pressure in a disproportionate way, bounce others into conclusions and communicate facts and opinions in a one-sided manner. Perhaps the best corrective to being manipulating is that most manipulators come off worst in the end!

WHAT MAKES A GOOD PERSUADER?

- Listening attentively and demonstrating that you have listened.
- Understanding clearly what matters most to the person you are trying to persuade.
- Having key facts available which underpin your argument.
- Aiming for win/win outcomes.
- Giving time to reflect to those you are seeking to persuade.
- Seeking new evidence and bringing it to the table without bouncing other people.
- Recognising the valid points and arguments of others.
- Being willing to adjust your argument while staying true to what you believe is right.

POINTS FOR REFLECTION

- When have you been at your best as an influencer or persuader and what approach did you take?
- Who have you observed trying to be manipulative and in what ways was their approach successful or counterproductive?
- In a forthcoming situation where you want to persuade others, what approach do you think is likely to be most successful?
- What are the potential drawbacks in relying on asking questions to enable others to reach their own conclusions, rather than seeking to overtly influence them?

Chapter 7
DETACHED OR DISENGAGED?

The football manager may well be physically separated from his players when the match is in progress, but he is not disengaged from the emotions of what is happening on the football pitch, whether his side is doing well or badly. If a football manager is both detached and disengaged, there is no energy or inspiration.

The 11-year-old boy is conscious of the cheering parents alongside the football pitch. Their engagement is uplifting. The parent who is both detached and disengaged and does not come to support their son is missing out on the pleasure of watching their son's efforts, and missing an opportunity to build a link with their child that can be carried forward into future years.

When a youngster takes an examination or goes for an interview, the parent is detached from the specific event. The supportive parent needs to be engaged by being fully supportive, while being disengaged so that their emotions do not get in the way of the youngster's efforts. Too much engagement and the youngster is stifled. Too little engagement and the youngster is starved of the emotional energy that is so important to enable them to grow into their full potential.

As a leader or manager, there is a balance between being detached or disengaged. A leader needs to be engaged with a team as it clarifies its objectives and values. But a degree of detachment is necessary so that the team becomes more confident in its own strengths and capacities. Once a team is established, the leader can be detached, watching from the grandstand.

The team leader needs to be engaged with the team to help build motivation. There will be a degree of disengagement from the detail as a team develops its own impact, but a good leader will never be completely disengaged. They will be acute enough to know when problems might arise and have a sense of when guidance might be needed. They might be viewing the action from the grandstand rather than the touchline, but there is an emotional engagement that ensures that there is a flow of interest and energy between the leader and the team on the pitch.

Joe was responsible for a project team that had a major initiative to deliver. Joe knew he had to remain detached and objective. He needed to understand how the project was viewed by a range of different people. He knew he must not become so immersed in the project that he became blinkered to some of the risks and potential shortcomings. John knew he had to disengage from some of the detail but he was determined not to become distanced from the project. He had invested a lot of emotional energy into getting the project agreed and setting it up.

Joe knew that he had to be careful that this emotional commitment did not undermine the objectivity with which he viewed the relative progress of the project. But his emotional engagement with the project was crucial: those working within the project needed to know that he cared. They needed to believe that Joe would back them in any difficult situation.

Joe was emotionally committed to the project and knew that it was important for the motivation of his people that this commitment was evident. He also recognised that a degree of disengagement was essential. He knew his emotions could be both a positive help and sometimes a dangerous explosive. Joe kept the balance right between engagement and disengagement through his involvement in other projects, through his conversation with trusted others and through his understanding of his own strengths and emotional reactions.

PRACTICAL WAYS OF BEING
CONSTRUCTIVELY DISENGAGED

- Keep a clear understanding of what success would look like.
- Ensure that you ask the advice of others who are observing your activity or project from a distance.
- Recognise the emotional triggers that can make you over anxious.
- Look ahead at the risks and be as objective as possible about them.
- If you begin to feel emotionally stressed about an issue, slow down and count to 10 before you do anything.
- Keep returning to what you believe is the next priority.

POINTS FOR REFLECTION

- How readily do you detach yourself when you need to and let others get on with the doing?
- Which are you more at risk of being: too disengaged or over engaged in projects?
- How best do you engage so that your energy motivates and inspires others?
- What are the practical steps that will enable you to disengage effectively, whilst still being able to decide when that is most important?

Chapter 8
BEING ENGAGED AND DETACHED AT THE SAME TIME

Members of a rugby team can be detached and engaged at the same time. They may be detached because the ball is elsewhere on the playing field. But they need to remain engaged so they are positioned correctly and alert if the ball comes to their section of the pitch. It is essential that the fullback remains engaged if the ball is in the opposition's half in readiness for a counter attack. The first lesson that a group of schoolboys learn when playing a team sport is not to spend all the time chasing the ball in whatever direction it goes.

A finance team in any organisation needs to be both engaged and detached. They need to keep a grip on the overall finance figures and understand trends, opportunities and risks. They need to be detached enough to allow those with day-to-day responsibility to have the accountability for the deployment and effective use of resources. If the finance team becomes too detached, they cease to have effective oversight of the use of the resources. If they are too engaged, they disenfranchise others, who will cease to be motivated to use the resources well.

The medical consultant needs to be engaged and detached at the same time. They need to be engaged enough to recognise a patient's symptoms while understanding the likely causes at the same time. They need to be detached enough to understand the emotional reactions of the patient and their family, while not being diverted from doing what is medically necessary.

Jenny was responsible for a customer service team in an insurance firm where the response times needed to improve. Jenny was clear in her own mind about the action that needed to be taken, but she had learnt from previous experience that just to tell the supervisors what to do and not engage with them was unlikely to lead to an improvement in performance. Jenny began a sequence of conversations with the supervisors to talk through the issues, discuss options that had been tried before, what the supervisors thought might be worth trying next and assess some of the opportunities and risks.

As a result of Jenny's engagement they arrived at a set of proposals that the supervisors were keen to implement. The supervisors then did a round of consultation with their staff, seeking their views on next steps. The resulting agreed approaches were not exactly what Jenny originally had in mind, but they were near enough and were likely to deliver the outcomes that would create the required improvement in performance.

Jenny had engaged with her people in developing next steps. She now wanted to keep a level of detachment that would enable her to assess whether the agreed action was delivering the needed results. She was emotionally committed to the action in hand, but recognised the risk of being too emotionally engaged, which could lead to a blinkered view of the progress made. Jenny knew that if progress was poor, then she would have to become more insistent about looking again at next steps.

The right balance between being engaged and detached will vary over time. If the level of involvement is always the same, it is likely that something is not quite right. Being deliberate about getting the balance right and sharing why you are changing your level of engagement gives signals that can help motivate others to raise their game.

A team that is working well is going to be fully engaged with delivering its objectives. It will also be able to sit outside itself and observe how the team is operating and the impact it is having.

BALANCING ENGAGEMENT AND DETACHMENT

- What are the risks if you become more detached?
- If you become more engaged, would this change be welcomed or resisted?
- Where is your natural inclination and do you need to make an adjustment because of that inclination?
- What is your intuition telling you is the right way to rebalance on this axis?
- If you made no change in your approach, what might be the consequences?

POINTS FOR REFLECTION

- Are there activities where you need to become more engaged?
- Are there other areas where you should become more detached?
- Do you get clear feedback about whether you are getting the balance right or wrong?

CONSIDER ONE SITUATION
YOU HAVE RESPONSIBILITY FOR:

- What are the outcomes you need to see delivered in six months?
- Where can you add most value in ensuring those outcomes are delivered?
- What are the main areas you need to be engaged with to ensure the outcomes are delivered?
- What type of detachment will ensure you keep your objectivity and enable others to take the lead in delivering progress?

PRINCIPLE AND PRAGMATISM

In some people's minds, describing an individual as pragmatic raises questions about their values, whereas for other people, to be described as pragmatic is a mark of admiration. One person's pragmatism is another person's lack of principle.

To be described as dominated by principles can either be a mark of respect for an individual's integrity, or an implied criticism that they are rigid and inflexible. In this section we ask: when is it all about principles; when is it all about pragmatism; when can principles get frozen in time; and when can balancing principles and pragmatism be the easy way out?

Chapter 9
WHEN IS IT ALL ABOUT PRINCIPLE?

When audit reports are drawn up, financial principles are applied. When reports are submitted about health and safety standards, judgements are made against a set of principles and standards. When a regulatory body makes a decision about the quality of a service and its value for money, they will have a set of principles or standards in mind when the judgements are made.

As individuals we have principles that are important to us in the way we work and in the way we balance our commitment between work, home and other activities.

If there is any suggestion of financial impropriety, there are clear principles against which judgements can be made. As a solicitor you apply principles drawn from legislation or legal practice. As an architect you are likely to follow certain principles that come from good architectural practice. As an engineer you are likely to follow clear scientific principles, such as recognising the significance of the law of gravity! Scientific principles are more readily accepted as absolute principles than other types of principles. Gravity always has a certain force. We cannot, for pragmatic reasons, reverse the pull of gravity. We can adapt to it and work around it, but we cannot change the force of gravity.

Increasingly, organisations have a clear set of principles that outline expected behaviour and conduct at work. Principles about respect for diversity have radically changed the willingness of minority groups to be open about their differences. Principles about behaviour have made it easier to recognise and deal with bullying in the workplace.

Joan was responsible for a product line in a food-processing factory. She was strict about applying principles of quality control and cleanliness. Being explicit about those principles made it easier to have clear expectations about principles of behaviour among the workforce. The principle of supporting each other by turning up on time and playing your full part was widely accepted. She knew that absolute consistency from her was important in ensuring that both quality control and codes of behaviour were applied consistently within the factory.

John spent many hours preparing his lectures at the university where he taught and was irritated when students turned up late. He exhorted the latecomers to try harder or teased them about their tardiness. Eventually he decided to apply a rigid rule of no access if students were late. Applying this principle made him unpopular with some, but it worked. After a while he relaxed this absolute principle when promptness levels improved. The pragmatic solution would have been to accept that a proportion of students would always be late but he wanted to make a point to see if he could modify the behaviour pattern of the students. His decision to be insistent on the principle of promptness changed behaviours and in his view was well worthwhile.

There is an obligation on each of us to be a whistleblower in the workplace where principles are being broken. This is perhaps easier to identify in terms of financial irregularity or the misuse of resources, but it potentially applies just as much to inappropriate behaviour and abuse of trust. What steps are we prepared to take when there is bullying, anger, insults or abuse in the workplace?

WHEN IS IT ALL ABOUT PRINCIPLE?

- Are legislative requirements being broken?
- Are financial rules or regulations being manipulated?
- Are an organisation's stated values and behaviours being ignored in a way that is damaging?
- Are there abuses of power and authority that mean individuals are not being treated fairly or consistently?
- Are there performance measures where results are being presented in an overly favourable way or being manipulated?

POINTS FOR REFLECTION

- What are the guiding principles that you are adamant you will adhere to?
- To what extent are your principles in the workplace about values, procedures or behaviours?
- How can you apply those principles in a more effective and consistent way and encourage others to do the same?

Chapter 10
WHEN IS IT ALL ABOUT PRAGMATISM?

Our days are full of pragmatic decisions. When the traffic light is green we have the right to drive across the intersection, but pragmatically we always have a careful look to see if there is another car coming from a different direction. We trust the people with whom we work to deliver their work on time, but pragmatically we might keep an eye on whether they are making the necessary progress. We do not believe that financial impropriety is going to happen within the organisation where we work, but we are reassured that there are effective audit arrangements in place to provide a check on whether financial disciplines are being followed.

Being pragmatic is recognising that human nature has a flexibility that means we are not always consistent or true to the principles that we articulate and most of the time believe are right. Human nature is infinitely adaptable, often for good but sometimes for ill. Being alert to that adaptability and pragmatism allows creative dialogue to happen so that new approaches can be developed to handle longstanding issues.

Pragmatism can be all about avoidance. The individual with an alcohol problem will do all they can to hide their addiction in a work context. They can become experts in deceit in order to hide their problem, with long-term consequences for the quality of the work they do. The individual for whom the bonus is a significant driver may have incentives to manipulate figures in order to get the best possible personal financial outcome.

On the other hand, being pragmatic is an important quality. The negotiator involved in settling a big contract will be applying a set of principles, but also knows that at a certain point they will need to be pragmatic about what deal is deliverable. The pay negotiator may have as their key principle "equal pay for work of equal value" but they know if they press the point too hard and insist on a significant pay increase, then the company is less likely to win financial orders, which will in turn put jobs at risk.

The construction company balances principles and pragmatism. There are clear principles about the design of a building, the building construction process, the health and safety standards to be met and the size of the building in order to meet planning requirements. But there is a pragmatism about the sequencing of the work, the workforce employed and the timetable. There can be a grey area about the quality of some of the materials used and some of the standards applied.

Sarah had been asked to provide a brief for her director of finance for a key meeting arranged at short notice. Sarah had a key set of principles in her mind about what a good-quality brief looked like but she recognised that the best could be the enemy of the good. Sarah had to be pragmatic. She only had half a day in which to prepare the brief, during which she was responding to other people's requests as well. Sarah's boss would read a brief of two pages properly, but anything longer he would skim superficially.

Sarah knew that for her brief to be of value she had to be pragmatic. She could not do all the research she wanted. She needed to identify a limited number of key points. She needed to put herself in her boss's position to understand what points he needed to know and what risks he needed to be aware of. Sarah produced the brief quickly and efficiently. It was fit for purpose but not perfect. The boss said the brief was helpful and clear. Sarah had made the right pragmatic decisions.

When Bob was invited to circulate his CV to see if other organisations would be willing to hire him, one or two friends suggested that he spend longer shaping his CV. He needed to be pragmatic and not rush into submitting his CV if it was unfinished. He needed to think about what people would read into his CV and the overall impact he wanted to have. Therefore, being pragmatic meant taking time to get the product right.

WHEN IS IT ALL ABOUT PRAGMATISM?

- How best do you handle situations where there are conflicting principles?
- When might following a principled line be counter-productive?
- When negotiating with others, at what point do you decide to be pragmatic after principles have been fully explained?
- How best do you watch whether individuals are being so pragmatic that they are likely to be undermining core principles?
- When for you might "the best be the enemy of the good"?
- How best do you test whether your own pragmatism is a positive quality or an avoidance strategy?

POINTS FOR REFLECTION

- In which situations are you applying principles where you need to be more pragmatic?
- Where, going forward, can pragmatism be an important part of your repertoire of competencies?

Chapter 11

WHEN CAN PRINCIPLES GET FROZEN IN TIME?

Mrs Cowgill was born in 1880 and throughout her life had been strict in her observance of Sundays as holy days. She enjoyed watching TV but did not watch it on Sundays because of her principles. During the 1960s her friends told her of the programme *Songs of Praise,* broadcast by the BBC on Sunday evenings. Reluctantly, she decided to break her principle of not expecting other people to work on Sundays and decided to watch this programme. As she moved into her 90s and was housebound this programme gave her immense joy. She had modified her principle and loved the inspiration which this programme gave her each Sunday evening.

Often we can apply principles in rather odd ways. Sometimes those people who do not buy a Sunday newspaper on principle will be avid readers of the Monday newspaper in order to catch up on the news. But the Sunday newspaper will have been written and printed on the Friday and Saturday, whereas the Monday newspaper will have been written and printed on a Sunday!

Sometimes we have no choice other than to reinterpret our principles. Was the Biblical edict strictly about working six days and observing one day of rest, or was it about creating a rhythm of life that included both work and rest? If the principle means literally six days working and one day off, that takes us in one direction. If the principle is about having a good balance between work and rest, that is a rather different starting point.

Rather than bemoaning the fact that we live in a world of instant communication and 24/7 activity, our survival depends on building in principles that will allow us to work effectively and have adequate rest and recuperation. Therefore, probably the ratio of 6:1 continues to be an appropriate principle but applied without necessarily having religious connotations.

We may believe that the quality of a product should always be at the same level, or that a career should be for life, or that divorce is wrong, or that seeking to move to another company is disloyal. But sometimes what we describe as a principle is more about personal preference. We sometimes use our chosen principles as a means of motivating ourselves or justifying a particular set of actions.

Henry believed that as an auditor he needed to apply strict principles. His view was that it was wrong to talk to a client in advance of doing an audit because he might be influenced by the views of the client. Henry believed he needed to bring strict objectivity. The consequence was that clients viewed him with suspicion and were unwilling to be open with him about some of the issues they faced. This made Henry's job more difficult as an auditor because he did not know the full background.

William took a very different view as an auditor. He wanted to build an understanding of the business and have a good relationship with company leaders. He wanted to understand the areas of concern. He wanted his clients to trust him enough to tell him in advance where there were problems. William saw his responsibility as being both an advisor and a policeman. He wanted to help the organisation produce accounts that were accurate and meaningful. He was absolutely clear about applying high standards in the audit, but he worked alongside the organisation and not in opposition to it. The result was that the quality of internal accounting improved because of the advice and recommendations he gave alongside the audit report.

Henry and William were both applying clear principles. Henry had a very traditional view of the auditor's relationship with the client. William was clear about the principles but recognised the importance of building the right relationships with key people in the organisation in order to do his job well.

The importance of building trust, having clear values, building quality relationships and putting effort and time into developing confidence in others are not things to be ignored. The way principles are demonstrated and recognised will change over time: living principles will be at the bedrock of both an individual's wellbeing and his or her relationships with co-workers.

WHEN CAN PRINCIPLES GET FROZEN IN TIME?

- Which are the principles that are most important to you in your life and work?
- How have those principles evolved over time?
- Which principles have been adapted to changing work, personal and family circumstances?
- Have you adapted your principles constructively or eroded them in a way you are less happy with?
- Is there any inconsistency between your personal views and your publicly expressed principles?
- To what extent is it useful that some principles are frozen in time?

POINTS FOR REFLECTION

- Are there principles that are important to you that have become frozen in time?
- Are there principles you have long held dear which need to be expressed in a different way?

Chapter 12

WHEN IS BALANCING PRINCIPLE AND PRAGMATISM THE EASY WAY OUT?

As human beings we are infinitely adaptable. We are always balancing our principles with pragmatic concerns. It is my right to cross the road here, but I am going to look out for any traffic that might be coming. It is right to spend time with individuals helping them develop and grow, but sometimes the time has to be cut short. It is important to place a high value on building key relationships, but that is not always possible in the way we want. Every project plan should be done to the highest possible standard, but sometimes you can only address a limited number of concerns in the time available. When I run workshops I want to apply the same level of personal engagement with each member of the team or group. But that is not always feasible.

We comfort ourselves by saying we have done all we can to balance principle and pragmatism, but does that mean we can duck important issues? We want someone to continue to be engaged on a particular project and therefore we may not tell them the frank truth about certain aspects of their contribution for fear that it will dampen their commitment.

We believe that a particular timetable is inviolate and, therefore, we continually make compromises even though we are doubtful about the consequences for the quality of the end product. We sense that people are losing interest in the project we are leading and then we justify our rather mediocre impact on others by saying we have had to balance principle and pragmatism.

Paul was leading a team where the motivation was mixed. Paul knew that pragmatically he had to keep this group motivated as much as possible. The quality of what they did was variable. He knew he had to tackle the performance issue and have some direct conversations. He was torn between applying some tough principles about standards, or adopting a pragmatic approach by motivating and encouraging his staff to keep going.

For a long time Paul dabbled with both approaches, promoting the need for high quality while also trying to encourage his people. He sensed that this had been the easy approach, but one that had not had much effect. Paul decided that he needed to tackle the performance and quality issues head on. He recognised that this would create a dip in motivation but he had concluded that he needed to be bold and apply clear principles about performance and quality. The result was an initial reaction of unhappiness amongst his staff. Two of them left but the others became more focused and the quality of their work improved. The lesson for Paul was that he had tried to balance principle and pragmatism for too long and needed to address the issues of principle directly and honestly.

Cynthia saw the relationship between principle and pragmatism as akin to the relationship between being strategic and tactical. Cynthia wanted to keep a careful focus on the long-term, strategic objectives while recognising that she had to be tactical in getting the agreement of a wide range of people. Cynthia recognised that there were moments where she was too tactical for her own good, and others began to regard her approach as manipulative. On the other hand, she knew that she needed to present the strategic objectives in a way that people thought were realistic.

Cynthia recognised that sometimes she had tried to balance the strategic and the tactical too subtly. She concluded that she needed to be explicit more often about the strategic objectives she was striving towards and the principles she was applying in order to achieve her aims. These needed to be the primary expression of her leadership, while recognising that being pragmatic and tactical had a supporting role to play.

WHEN IS BALANCING PRINCIPLE AND PRAGMATISM THE EASY WAY OUT?

- How conscious are you of balancing principle and pragmatism in the decisions you make?
- When has it been helpful to recognise how you are balancing principle and pragmatism?
- When has an attempt to balance principle and pragmatism meant that your message or impact has become unclear?
- In what circumstances has it been helpful to focus strongly on principles rather than pragmatism?
- When has being purely pragmatic let you down badly?
- How do you handle a situation where your sense of the right thing to do is not in line with trying to find a balance between principle and pragmatism?
- How best do you get the balance right between strategic and tactical aims?

POINTS FOR REFLECTION

- Are there current situations where the way you might balance principle and pragmatism can create a straightforward but not necessarily preferable way out?
- In what situations do you now need to decide to either apply principle more strongly or be more pragmatic?

AWARENESS AND ACTION

There is a delicate balance between awareness and action. You want to keep alert to what is happening around you. You want to be attuned to understand the trends and the politics. But you do not want to be bludgeoned into action. You want to be aware of what is going on, but without being over-anxious. You want to be ready to take action when needed and when the timing is right. You want to combine a lightness of touch with a clarity of thought about what is going on around you.

This section looks in turn at what happens when you stop listening, watching your impact, picking the right moment for action, and keeping a virtuous circle of action and awareness. Knowing when to act and when to withdraw may involve many subtleties, as you keep alert to what is happening around you.

Chapter 13
WHEN YOU STOP LISTENING YOU DIE

The one-year-old child does not speak but does a lot of observing and listening. The youngster's head moves when they hear different sounds. They smile when they recognise the voice of a parent, or even a grandparent. They are hearing the tone of voice as much as the content. The voice that sounds a bit harsh can lead to tears, even when the words are perfectly loving. The youngster is picking up signals all the time and using that to decide who to trust and how to respond.

The teenager may be creating lots of noise that others have to listen to. The sounds of contemporary music may become almost addictive, whereas listening to parents might be seen as something to be avoided. Teenagers are often listening while being determined to give a visual impression of blankness or disdain. During what may be turbulent teenage years, the parent knows they have to keep observing and listening, with any action being tempered by an awareness of teenage sensitivities.

The young manager or professional who is doing well is absorbing the experience of others. A junior doctor needs to listen attentively to the wisdom of the consultant. The young teacher gleans from the experience of others and observes how they handle difficult situations or demanding pupils. The young manager listens to understand what the boss needs, some of which will be articulated clearly, while other elements will be implied.

The individual in the second half of life may have a huge amount of expertise and experience to offer. But if it is just delivered as from a podium the words become hot air that soon fades. The influential person in the second half of their life is one who listens intently to what is going on around them and senses when and how to contribute, having understood others' point of view.

The older person who becomes entrenched in their own world and stops asking questions or showing they are listening to others will still be cherished by family and friends; but if the two-way engagement is lost, the bonds of affection become based on what was and not what is now. When someone stops listening, something dies in the relationship.

The Diocese of Guildford has a training programme for pastoral assistants to which I contribute a session on the skill of conversation. The starting point is always about listening well. The good pastoral assistant will be listening with both their ears and their eyes. They will be alert to what is said and not said. They will be sensing all the emotions, including both pain and joy. They will be alert to jerky movements and any sense of unease. They will allow silence to happen so that the individual can be reflecting back and processing their thoughts. The pastoral assistant who is listening well will be letting the individual both think, talk and reflect, with the act of listening being a process of encouragement and engagement in which the listener may say very few words.

Carolyn was adept at listening and observing at the start of the meeting. She was listening to the tone of voice as people entered the room. She was listening to the tone set by the chairperson and the visual reactions of her colleagues. She knew whose contributions would uplift and stretch the thinking of colleagues, and whose might create a sense of boredom. She knew if she stopped listening her contributions would be less effective, but if she just listened and did not contribute at all, then perhaps the listening was wasted.

WHAT MAKES A GOOD LISTENER?

- Observe the physical movements as well as listening to the words.
- Recognise how an individual's words are influenced by their cultural background, education and role in the organisation.
- Look for the emotions behind the words.
- Give someone your sole, undivided attention so they do not feel inhibited in what they say.
- Create a sense of trust so that the individual can say what they think.
- Allow space and silence and don't feel you have to rush in with a comment.
- Ask open-ended questions that demonstrate you have heard.
- Crystallize some of what you have heard in short phrases so it is obvious that you have listened.
- Hold back your own opinions until the other person is ready to hear other views.
- Demonstrate that you want to engage and don't dismiss the perspective of others.
- Look as if you are enjoying the conversation.

POINTS FOR REFLECTION

- Who has listened to you well over recent weeks and why did you reach that view?
- Which frame of mind, body posture, and context helps you listen best?
- How best do you demonstrate that you are listening and not just going through the motions?

THINK FORWARD TO SOME
CONVERSATIONS YOU NEED TO HAVE:

- What are you listening for in those conversations?
- How will you demonstrate that you are listening?
- How will you ensure that the pace of the conversation is conducive to the needs of the person you are talking with?

Chapter 14

WATCH YOUR IMPACT

Amanda saw herself as an energetic and enthusiastic contributor who was full of ideas. She always wanted to contribute and felt that she could move discussions constructively forward on most subjects. Amanda's self-perception was that colleagues wanted her around because of her energy and ideas, and that every conversation or project would be better because of her contribution.

Amanda's colleagues were not quite as convinced. They liked her brightness and respected her energy. But her relentlessness was exhausting. Her constant talking was debilitating to others. Her apparent pushiness meant that her colleagues sought to avoid her, and were not always ready to listen with openness and patience to what she said.

When Amanda got some feedback that she should tone her contribution down she was shocked and felt hurt. Why would anybody not respond well to her passion and energy? She was contributing so much and now felt under-appreciated, but the advice of friends began to sink in. She needed to be mindful of her impact. What mattered was not what she said but whether anyone listened to or engaged with what she said. If the words and energy made no difference, she might as well have not bothered in the first place.

Amanda began to think about what she wanted to achieve from different discussions. As a middle manager in a local government authority, her colleagues could choose to ignore her. She did not have the status and power of the senior people. Amanda needed to capture people's interest and imagination.

Amanda wanted to develop a joint project with a local health authority. Her first instinct was to tell the people in the health authority that they needed to co-operate. Amanda recognised that such a didactic approach was unlikely to win active co-operation. She had to work with her colleagues in the health authority to build a shared view about the outcomes they wanted to reach and the benefits for both the local authority and the health authority. It was a step-by-step process of listening hard, with Amanda recognising the impact that she could have on others. Amanda accepted that sometimes she had to bide her time until her colleagues were ready to move to the next step. Amanda grew increasingly conscious that her impact depended on building a sense of emotional engagement and rapport just as much as on the content and quality of her arguments.

Which speakers engage you most? The speaker who fires our imagination and has an impact on our thinking is usually someone who can catch our interest through the stories they tell; they show an understanding of the issues we face or the questions in our mind. The effective speaker comes over as recognising our needs and concerns. We feel a sense of trust, allegiance and shared perspective. The speaker who has an impact is rarely someone who harangues us about our failings or sends us into gloom or guilt. The speaker who gets results captures our imagination, inspiring us by what is possible, and energises us to take positive steps.

Observing our own reactions to the demands, overtures or requests of others provides a valuable indicator of what type of approaches have a constructive impact, and which have a counter-productive effect. Using our own reactions as an indicator of the impact someone is having and giving feedback in a timely and constructive way can be so valuable to others. Providing feedback is often best done away from the heat of the moment. Feedback can be more objective when the emotions have passed.

BEING ALERT TO YOUR IMPACT ON OTHERS

- Reflect after events when you have been influential and when you have been less influential.
- When are you most effective at energising others?
- When are you most effective at enabling people to be creative?
- When do people appear to shy away from talking with you?
- When do you need to hold off and give someone the opportunity to respond without making the same point for the third time?
- How do you best stand back and decide what is the most important long-term impact you want?
- How best do you create a win/win situation, where success for both parties is recognised and acknowledged?
- How easily do you accept a situation where you might have had an important influence and all the credit goes to someone else?
- How alert are you to the risk of seeking an impact that is about your success rather than the greater good?
- How readily can you enjoy the successes of others and not need approval for the contribution you have made?

POINTS FOR REFLECTION

- When has your impact been the opposite of what you intended and why did that happen?
- When were you particularly influential and what did you do that led to that result?
- Where do you want to have a particular impact and what steps do you want to take to maximise the prospect of that outcome?

Chapter 15
WHEN IS THE MOMENT FOR ACTION?

When a group of people have different views and are working through an issue there can be a moment in time when an astute participant senses exhaustion with the repeated arguments and sees an embryonic desire to find a way through. This can be the moment for summarising the debate so far and suggest a way forward. Participants may be ready to accept that they will not get their ideal outcome and that now is the moment to reach a consensus on next steps. A suggested way forward introduced earlier in the conversation is likely to have been met with disinterest. But left until much later in the debate, participants might be too exhausted to hear a potential way through.

Timing is all. You get the timing right, and progress can be made quickly. You get the timing wrong, and you might as well not have bothered.

Sometimes the moment for action is dictated by external circumstances. The lease for the building is running out and a decision has to be made by a certain time. The loan for an investment has to be paid back by a certain date. If no action is taken the banks will be scrutinising the figures. The young, fresh-faced 30-year-old who readily approved the loan for the organisation will be all over the company accounts, possibly bringing a self-righteous and disapproving manner.

On other occasions the risk is thinking that the action can always wait until tomorrow. You hope the individual whose performance has been indifferent will get better. You believe that people will improve and recover from bad patches. You are always optimistic. The risk is that difficult conversations are put off again and again. The result is that the action becomes more difficult as the situation becomes increasingly acute and the individual is oblivious to the problem.

Henry was conscious that one of the senior leaders working under him, called Len, was not as effective as he used to be. Henry felt a debt to Len as Len had encouraged him in the early stages of his career. Henry did not want to humiliate Len. He genuinely believed that Len was going through a bad patch and would find his energy and verve again. But Len's performance continued to be indifferent: his staff were limited in their effectiveness and not very motivated. Henry allowed himself to become blinkered to some of the problems in Len's area and put a brave face on what was happening.

The rude awakening for Henry was when his own boss kept questioning Len's performance. Henry did not sound convincing either to his boss or to himself. Eventually, Henry decided he had to take action. He faced up to the need to have an honest conversation with Len. Len was critical of Henry's management style, but acknowledged that his own performance had not been as good as he wanted. He accepted that he needed to make changes. Henry was optimistic, but perhaps too optimistic.

The reality was that Len did not change his approach much. His staff remained dissatisfied and the outcomes continued to be indifferent. Henry knew the time had come for a firmer conversation with performance measures put in place. Entering this conversation felt traumatic for Henry but he knew he had to take action. There were cross words and eventually Len left the organisation. Henry and Len shook hands on the final day, but it was a formal farewell with little warmth between them.

Henry had accepted that he needed to take action for the good of the organisation, its staff and its customers. It was a painful lesson for Henry that had he acted earlier the outcome might have been different. He needed good friends to remind him that Len had created the situation where action was needed. Len's underperformance and lack of commitment was, at the end of the day, Len's problem and not Henry's.

WHEN DO YOU JUDGE THE MOMENT FOR ACTION?

- Is your default position to act too quickly or too slowly?
- From your own experience, when have you got the timing right and what did you learn from this?
- What helps you take action when you are hesitant to do so?
- What helps you get into the right frame of mind to take the necessary action when you are feeling hesitant?
- How do you judge whether your action is bold enough?
- How do you ensure you get feedback from those who can assess objectively whether your action is working?
- How do you hold back when emotionally you want to act now but rationally you know you need to bide your time?

POINTS FOR REFLECTION

- What might be holding you back from taking the action you need to?
- How best will you judge when the timing is right to intervene?
- Who are you going to talk with to help you clarify whether now is the right moment to act?

Chapter 16

KEEPING A VIRTUOUS CIRCLE OF ACTION AND AWARENESS

The pilot of an aeroplane balances awareness and action. The awareness comes through their experience of what is working smoothly or less smoothly. The awareness is informed by the data that is available in the cockpit. The pilot is aware of the reactions of the co-pilot and can take a second opinion. The responsibility for action is clear. The pilot has to get the aeroplane safely to its destination with no disruption to the passengers. But the pilot has been trained to think about when contingent action is needed.

Sometimes, action is planned carefully, such as when dealing with turbulence. Sometimes the pilot has to react quickly to a flock of birds or a flash of lightning. Awareness and action are inextricably linked for the pilot. The virtuous circle consists of preparedness and readiness for action, with an openness to the range of different contingencies that a pilot needs to be prepared to handle.

Driving a car at night can be unnerving on an unfamiliar road. We like to be aware of what is happening around us and of the risks ahead. But in the dark, when we cannot see the street names or the direction of the road more than 50 yards ahead, we can become unnerved because the information available to us is partial. Our limited awareness can make us either apprehensive about driving at night in new places, or make us acutely aware of the need to plan ahead and work out a route in advance. People who enjoy driving at night have taught themselves to focus on the key bits of information they need to drive safely in the dark and then be prepared to take action when unexpected bends appear.

As a teacher, Rosalind was adept at balancing awareness and action. She could sense the mood of her pupils, knowing when they needed to be physically active and when they were ready to be quiet and draw or read. She had an acute sense of their level of engagement and their risk of boredom, which enabled her to decide on appropriate activities. Within any one teaching period, she would be responding to a range of different moods. She needed to create a virtuous circle because she wanted the pupils to look forward to their lessons and have confidence in her as a teacher who could handle their moods well and enable them to learn.

For a schoolteacher, balancing awareness and action may happen every few minutes. When a doctor sees a patient in a surgery, they may take three minutes to build an awareness of the health issue and two minutes to decide and implement an action. The medical consultant may initiate a number of tests before deciding on the action needed.

Balancing awareness and action is something we do every day in assessing and making small decisions. We accept that when making bigger, strategic decisions or ones that involve significant expenditure, much more time is needed before action can be taken.

What can help create a virtuous circle is being clear about the kind of data needed before good decisions can be taken. Sometimes, gathering more and more information can be a means of avoiding or putting off a problem. On other occasions, more data is key to reaching a successful outcome. Being selective about what further data is needed is not always straightforward. Sometimes, "the best" can be the enemy of "the good" in seeking ever more perfect information, when the time has come to make the best possible decision on the basis of the insight and information available to us.

KEEPING A VIRTUOUS CIRCLE
OF ACTION AND AWARENESS

- Who do you observe getting this balance right?
- When is there the risk that you seek further information as a means of putting off a decision?
- Can you recognise when you might want to rush in to make a decision when you might be better observing for longer before deciding?
- What techniques help you be aware of the intentions and emotions of those around you?
- What can you learn from observing others in different spheres who have to balance action and awareness?
- What can derail you from getting the balance right between awareness and action, and how do you handle these derailers?

POINTS FOR REFLECTION

- How are you balancing awareness and action in your work and personal life?
- If you are balancing action and awareness better in some areas than others, what can you learn from this experience?
- How might you re-adjust the relationship between awareness and action in some areas of your life?

RATIONAL AND EMOTIONAL

We are both rational and emotional beings. Sometimes we strive to be completely rational. On other occasions our emotional responses come to the fore and can dominate our reactions. Sometimes our rational and emotional responses can be aligned, and on other occasions, markedly different. There is a wonderful line in the film *The Iron Lady* when Mrs Thatcher, the UK prime minister, is reported as being irritated by the emphasis on how people feel when, what matters, she says, is how they think and act. But acting without any regard to how people feel is likely to produce an overly negative response that is often counter-productive.

This section explores using emotions as valuable data, becoming too rational for your own good, keeping your emotional and rational reactions in tune with each other, and keeping alert to all that is happening within you.

Chapter 17
USING YOUR EMOTIONS AS VALUABLE DATA

The way the brain is constructed means that emotional responses happen much faster than rational responses. The brain reacts emotionally to events before we have had a chance to process them. It operates on the basis of minimising danger and fires up more intensively when it perceives a threat. Sometimes it fires up when it perceives a threat that is similar to a previous bad experience, even though the events might be quite different.

We all have emotional triggers stored in the limbic system in our brain. These emotional triggers may be linked with a project or presentation that went wrong, a bruising encounter or a crisis where everyone panicked. The danger is that a negative emotional response kicks in when something apparently similar happens and reduces the resources available for rational thought.

The aroused limbic system looks out for dangers, often interpreting events negatively. Quick, emotional responses may mean positive stimuli are missed. The "flight or fight" reaction kicks in, the emotions are heightened and our rational impulse can be suppressed and hidden.

Our emotional reactions can be unhelpful or get in the way. We may take a comment personally when no slight was intended. We feel emotional about an issue, speak too soon and too quickly, and do not carry people with us. We are aggrieved about an action someone has taken and show our frustration. We say critical words in the moment without thinking of their consequences. We can enter some situations feeling fear, with the consequence that our energy is drained and it is difficult to view a discussion calmly and in a measured way.

Sometimes our emotional reactions bring to the surface irrational fears. We believe our whole world is going to collapse if one small thing goes wrong, or we can feel like a victim, criticised and ignored by others. When we go into victim mode and celebrate our own martyrdom, we are at risk of our negative emotions quashing the life, energy and desires within us.

But our emotional reactions are crucial to our survival and success. Primitive people needed the early warning that came through emotional reactions so that they could fight or flee in the face of danger. We all know of moments of fear when we have moved out of the way of on-coming traffic very quickly. Feelings of apprehension, unease or fear provide valuable data that stops us risking life and limb.

Apprehension about individuals or a sense of wariness can provide valuable data about who to trust and who to handle with care. Uneasy feelings about a forthcoming meeting might be an indication that we need to prepare carefully for it. Reacting crossly about the outcome of a discussion might mean that the issue is not yet resolved and more work needs to be done before a final resolution can be reached.

William was going to lead a team delivering on a contract for a big, commercial organisation. William was excited but after meeting a number of people and doing research about the role, he felt a mixture of emotions. This included emotions of expectation and excitement, but there were also feelings of apprehension and unease.

William wanted to use his emotions as valuable data. He decided that the best way to do this was to talk to a good friend and try to stand back from his own emotions. William wanted to understand the sources of his positive emotions and ensure that these emotions continued to give him energy and resolve. He wanted to understand how much of his feelings of apprehension and unease were part of the normal process of moving into a new role.

William became conscious that some of his fears came from what he was picking up from conversations and observations. He sensed instinctively there were problems that needed to be addressed. Through discussions with trusted friends, William began to clarify those issues and recognised that his emotions had not been random, but had been warning him of issues he needed to be mindful of. The secret for William was sitting outside his emotions and trying to understand what message they were giving him about both himself and the situation he was about to enter.

WAYS OF INTERPRETING YOUR EMOTIONAL REACTIONS

- Sit outside yourself and practice noticing what is happening to you.
- Name the emotion you are feeling.
- Recognise your habitual emotional patterns.
- Reframe the emotion if it is a negative one: i.e., recognise that is helpful to have an early warning of a potential problem.
- Reflect on what a third party would notice and what advice they would give you.
- What advice would you give to someone else having similar emotional reactions?
- Who are the trusted others you can discuss your feelings with?
- How best can you allow your rational side to catch up with the emotional?

- When an emotional reaction is very strong, can you mentally move into a different space and deliberately focus your attention away from that reaction?

POINTS FOR REFLECTION

Examine some issues you are dealing with at the moment:
- Are there emotional reactions that give you helpful insights?
- Are there emotional reactions that get in the way of you addressing issues?
- If you regard your emotions as providing valuable data, to what extent do your emotional responses enable you to interpret the situation clearly?

Chapter 18

WHEN CAN YOU BE TOO RATIONAL FOR YOUR OWN GOOD?

Geoffrey prided himself on being able to sort out every problem in a rational way. His method was to dissect every problem into a sequence of steps and approach it with the firm belief that there was a solution for each step.

Geoffrey's belief was that through cool, calm thought and reflection you could solve any problem. If there was an issue he would find a quiet space, get a blank sheet of paper and write down the key facts and considerations. He took the view that he needed to work up three options in order to look objectively at the merits of each. He would then take a separate sheet of paper and identify the key risks of each. He would score each risk on a one-to-ten scale and identify some of the most effective ways of tackling those risks. He would use this data to decide which of the options was the most appropriate next step.

Geoffrey prided himself on his logical and rational approach. He had been inspired by courses he had been on dealing with project management. His approach was admired by colleagues, but his careful, methodical manner irritated some and did not bring out the best in others. Geoffrey had a reflective character and needed to work through problems alone. Other colleagues preferred to talk issues through before reaching conclusions about next steps.

Felicity responded well to Geoffrey's style. She was an accountant and very rational in her approach. Commercial considerations came first. From Felicity's perspective, the crucial element in any decision was the financial data: her ideal activity was poring over spreadsheets. Felicity recognised the importance of the financials. Unless the figures showed that the project was worthwhile, there was no point in proceeding, but the likely success of the project depended on the emotional reactions of so many people. For the project to succeed there needed to be a level of motivation and commitment that would see the team work successfully through difficult and demanding periods. This was not going to be a linear exercise in which what mattered was the rational assertion that the right steps were being taken. There needed to be a strong sense of shared endeavour, emotional commitment and belief in each other's contribution for the project to be successful.

In a different organisation Ron had been asked to devise new pay arrangements that would be suitable for the next phase of the organisation's development. He approached the task rationally and produced a complex set of arrangements that recognised a wide range of different contributions and linked business development and delivery of figures in a precise way to remuneration. It was a perfectly formed edifice. It tried to address the likely behaviour of individuals and as a consequence, became more and more complex.

Ron's proposals were beautifully rational and logical. The risk was they would be incomprehensible to many, distort behaviour patterns, and encourage people to compete with each other and be continually focused on their own personal bottom line. The alternative was a much simpler model that would include elements of rough justice but which most people were willing to buy into.

Most employees felt that the sophisticated model Ron had created was a masterpiece of theory which would be destructive in practice. Ron recognised why the majority did not favour his approach and understood the emotional reasons why there was hesitancy about accepting his sophisticated model. He reluctantly accepted that, perhaps, he was being too rational. He accepted that clarity, simplicity and the motivational effect on team behaviour rather than individual competitiveness were important considerations that he had not given enough attention to.

Clearly understanding the rational arguments is normally the right starting point for any difficult decision, but information is not just about facts. It needs to cover data about the likely reaction of individuals and groups. Information about emotional reactions is just as valid as information about finance.

HOW DO YOU ASSESS WHETHER YOU ARE BEING TOO RATIONAL FOR YOUR OWN GOOD?

- When in the past has a rational approach been helpful and when has it meant you have missed a key consideration?
- Is your natural tendency to be swayed by the rational or the emotional?
- How best do you assess the likely emotional reactions of yourself, the people you work with and customers in order to be clear what arguments are likely to be most influential?
- How do you best test whether you are being one dimensional in bringing a purely rational approach?
- Who will give you feedback about whether you are being too rational to be effective?

POINTS FOR REFLECTION

- What will enable you to think as clearly and as rationally as possible about the issues you are currently handling?
- How best do you build into that assessment an objective view about emotional reactions and interpretations?
- How best do you take people with you so that you do not become isolated and ignored?

Chapter 19

KEEPING YOUR EMOTIONAL AND RATIONAL REACTIONS IN TUNE WITH EACH OTHER

Our rational and emotional reactions are rarely in time with each other. Often, the emotional reaction will kick in before the rational reaction – hence the value of sleeping on an issue to let the unconscious do some thinking so that the rational can catch up with the emotional. Most of us have had the experience of waking up in the morning with a clear sense of the right next step in addressing an issue, which on the previous evening had seemed insoluble. The brain needs time to process what it is learning and draw on previous experience. Perhaps, too, the brain seeks to understand an issue within the context of our values and beliefs so that the resulting thought process takes account of the range of influences from our experience and insight.

On other occasions the emotional reaction can continue for a long time after rationally we have moved on. We may be in a new role, with our rational thought processes focusing on doing the new job well. But there might be some emotional throwback to a previous job. There might be a hankering for the emotional support that was part of a previous role, or there might be a continuing sense of frustration or unfairness when we felt that we had been treated badly in the previous role. We can become stuck in time, caught up in the emotions of a previous experience, with a reluctance to move on and let the past be the past, even though our rational self has moved on.

After a close family member or friend dies, the grieving process can take a couple of years. The emotional reaction after the termination of a job you enjoyed can take a similar length of time. Marcia had been an executive director of a subsidiary for three years. The results had been good and she felt she was on a pathway to promotion. But a new chief executive had been appointed to the holding company whose style was markedly different.

Marcia tried hard to impress, perhaps too much. The new chief executive did not regard Marcia as strategic enough to lead the organisation. She was asked to move sideways into another role with less responsibility. Marcia felt aggrieved but tried not to show her crossness. Marcia knew that she had to be utterly professional and hold her head up high. She needed to be positive with her staff about her successor and what the future held for them.

Inside Marcia was boiling, but she kept her cool. Marcia needed to let her emotional reactions out. Her partner was wise enough to realise that he had to absorb some of Marcia's angst over a couple of months. Marcia moved on rationally quite quickly and began to enjoy her new role, but emotionally it still rankled within her that she had been "demoted". The grief process had to take its course and needed more time than she had expected. Eventually, she was able to say to her former boss that the move to a different part of the organisation had been right for both her and the company.

It is inevitable that our emotional and rational reactions will be out of step with each other. They are not the equivalent of the right and left foot, happily operating in tandem. Our rational reactions may be more predictable than our emotional reactions.

Sometimes understanding can come through keeping one foot firmly on the ground while observing the movement of the other foot. Sometimes our rational and emotional reactions seem discordant and have a different underlying beat. We may have to accept that we need to try to build rhythms where the rational and emotional reactions reinforce each other rather than being mutually destructive.

KEEPING YOUR EMOTIONAL AND RATIONAL REACTIONS IN TUNE WITH EACH OTHER

- Observe the cycles of your emotional reactions so you are not upset by them quite so much in the future.
- Accept that sometimes the emotional reaction is very quick and on other occasions painfully slow.
- Allow yourself to sleep on issues where there is apparent discordance.
- When you are in danger of becoming fixated on a particular view, allow yourself to be open to new information or insights.
- Recognise which of the reactions – emotional or rational – is dominant, and be willing to make some adjustments to take account of that reaction.

POINTS FOR REFLECTION

- Can you assess the extent to which your rational and emotional reactions are in tune with each other?
- If there is discordance, why is that happening, and to what extent is it sapping your energy?
- What could be done to reduce this discordance and bring your emotional and rational reactions in harmony with each other?

Chapter 20

BEING AWARE OF ALL THAT IS HAPPENING INSIDE YOU

We are a cacophony of reactions. Looking at ourselves is like looking through a kaleidoscope, where sometimes the colours are random and on other occasions they fit into a neat pattern.

When I begin to work with someone as a coach I seek to understand their family and cultural background. Many of our perspectives and reactions were formed in our childhood and youth. Whether we like it or not, our parents live on in us through the conditioning of elements of our behaviour and attitudes.

Often, the first impression we give to others is very different to what is happening inside us. The bravado exhibited by some is a cover for their lack of confidence. Beneath the reserve of others there is a creative mind ready to burst out with new ideas and approaches. Beneath the gentleness of a lady who looks as if a light wind would blow her over is a crystal clear mind and a tough approach to addressing any problem. For some, inside the velvet glove there is an iron fist. For others, inside the chainmail glove there is a soggy marshmallow.

Our heritage and personal history may have a firm grip upon us, but we are never completely captive to our past. We always have choices in the way we interpret events. We may sometimes feel that we are not able to make decisions, but every day we make decisions about our attitude and can influence what is happening within us.

Being mindful of what is happening within us can give us powerful data: when we feel excited about a forthcoming piece of work, this gives us reassuring messages about our competence and about our confidence in tackling particular situations. When we feel nervous, that provides us with an alertness to handle new situations well; but nerves can mean we are on edge and not as effective as we would like to be.

We may observe in ourselves changing attitudes to different situations. Our appetite for risk will change depending on our roles and our reputation, as well as on our personal financial status. When someone's children become financially independent, the parent might feel liberated in lots of ways, including being more willing to express their views in the workplace and be less worried about the possibility of losing their job.

What is happening within us may well be an interaction between our beliefs about life and people, alongside the opportunities and constraints of the work we are in. The areas in which we would like to make a difference may change significantly over time. Our passion in the early part of our career might be to have a focused, personal impact. Later on, we might measure success more through the impact of our whole team. Later still, the measure might be more related to our ability to develop leadership qualities in other people.

Observing the energy levels within can be a valuable source of data not only about ourselves but of the team as a whole. Emotional states are contagious. If we are feeling flat and unadventurous, others are likely to be in the same mood. If we exude a positive attitude in the workplace, it can be infectious. If we are feeling drained, others are likely to follow suit.

Pamela was very conscious that she could have an acute emotional reaction to people and situations. Sometimes this could distort her approach and create parallel, emotional reactions in others. She knew she had to get a grip on some of her emotional responses. The way she did this was to set time aside to talk through with two or three trusted others the emotions going on inside her. This way, she was able to distinguish when these emotions provided useful data, when they were historic legacies and when they were just noise in the system.

KEEPING ALERT TO ALL THAT IS HAPPENING WITHIN YOU

- Sit outside yourself and observe your emotions.
- Recognise the continuing influence of family and cultural background on your thoughts, responses and behaviour.
- Be amused by what emotional reactions you can become captive to.
- Try to separate out your reactions, useful insights and background noise.
- When you feel a sense of lightness, enjoy the sensation and be open to where it might lead you.
- When you feel stagnant, reflect on what lifts your spirits.
- When you feel hyperactive, remember what calms you down.
- When you are bored, remember what catches your imagination.

POINTS FOR REFLECTION

- What, at the moment, is burning within you?
- Which hopes and aspirations are dominant?
- What are the fears that can get in the way?
- What new insight or reassuring messages are coming from within you?

INDIVIDUAL AND COLLECTIVE

When two people play tennis doubles together there is a responsibility on both individuals to play well and to act in tandem. The individualist will rarely be an outstanding doubles player whereas the contestant who can enhance the quality of his or her partner's performance so that the outcome is more than the sum of the parts will blossom when playing doubles.

Rarely does success come purely from the actions of the individual. We are normally part of a group or team where success flows from a shared purpose and complementary contributions. This section asks: when is it your problem and no one else's; what is it only you can do; where do your family and friends fit in; and when does the team come first?

Chapter 21

WHEN IS IT YOUR PROBLEM AND NO ONE ELSE'S?

If one member of a tennis doubles pair loses her form, her partner will want to encourage and motivate her so that her good form returns. But, ultimately, it is the responsibility of the player whose performance has dipped to get her sharpness back and perform at the top level. The individual doing a rock climb is dependent on his colleagues for his safety. But it is for the individual himself to maintain the resolve and use the best techniques to reach the summit.

Ben worked with a sequence of government ministers as a parliamentary clerk. It was Ben's job to ensure that parliamentary questions were answered expeditiously and accurately. He built up a fearsome reputation, but on one occasion he did not transpose some figures accurately into the final answer, which when published in Hansard resulted in press criticism and an unhappy minister. Ben's first reaction was to want to hide, but he knew he had to take responsibility and own up to his mistake. He could have blurred the details of what happened, but decided that it was his problem and he needed to be honest about it. The minister respected him for admitting the mistake and shrugged his shoulders saying, "These things happen". Ben knew that his future reputation depended on not making the same mistake again.

Geraldine was leading a project to put a new IT system in place by a particular date. There was a clear project plan, lots of impressive charts and a risk assessment that the auditors thought was outstanding. All was well for the first few months, then a couple of key people left and the suppliers did not quite meet some milestones. There was a request for some relatively minor specification changes and the costs looked to be going up. Geraldine was thorough in tackling each of these issues. None of the problems were her fault, but in combination they began to look quite acute.

Geraldine explained to her boss that these were a sequence of problems that other people needed to solve. Her boss looked her in the eye and said, "They are your problems because you are accountable for the success of the project." This firm rejoinder was a reminder to Geraldine that she could not pass accountability on to other people: ultimate accountability was hers. The consequence was that Geraldine reflected hard on what were the right actions to ensure progress was made with each of the individual problems, while ensuring that the detail was a matter for other people to solve. Geraldine needed to achieve a subtle balance. She recognised that she had accountability for the overall project and it was her problem if there was a failure in one area. At the same time, she needed to ensure that those responsible for individual areas focussed on finding solutions and did not dump their problems on her.

When I first became the Finance Director General for a government department I inherited significant overspending in one area. When we talked to the Secretary of State about what she wanted to do about the problem, she was firm that it was our job to find a solution. She was willing to make difficult decisions in due course, but was clear that the problem should be addressed and solutions explored by officials first. We eventually found a way through and resolved the issue without having to pass the problem on to the minister.

WHEN IS IT YOUR PROBLEM AND NO ONE ELSE'S?

- How much ultimate accountability do you carry?
- To what extent has a problem arisen because of your own actions?
- Are you in a position where you can help find a solution even though individual issues are more directly the concern of others?
- How strongly is there an expectation on you to be the problem solver?
- What is likely to happen if you do nothing?
- What does your conscience say is your ultimate accountability?
- How might you dissect the problem so it does not look so daunting?
- What are the potential next steps to solving the problem?

POINTS FOR REFLECTION

- Is there an issue that you need to accept as your problem and find a solution, or orchestrate others in finding a solution?
- Are there instances where you are shifting responsibility to others but where you need to accept that it is your problem?
- What is your usual pattern: do you tend to pass problems too much on to other people, or do you tend to embrace them as yours alone?
- How might you get the balance right between ensuring others feel a sense of responsibility and you owning the overall problem?

Chapter 22

WHAT IS IT ONLY YOU CAN DO?

Living leadership means nurturing and growing the energy of both the individual and the team. Both are crucial for success. Most leaders can see where they can make a difference. They want to add value in lots of different ways. They may be better equipped than many of their team to do individual tasks well, but asking "What is the value I can bring?" may be the wrong question. A better question might be: "What is it only I can do?" This applies a tougher filter on how best a leader uses their time and energy.

In a football team the goalkeeper is the only player who can use their hands to stop the ball inside the penalty area. In a cricket match, when the bowler is running up to bowl only the batsman at the crease is allowed to hit the ball.

Robin was very good at drafting submissions to ministers. He could write clearly and crystallize key arguments. He got enormous pleasure from crafting a submission that was clear and insightful, giving the pros and cons of different options. Such was his skill that virtually all the submissions for ministers from his department were written by him. But was this the best use of his time and energy? Could he teach others to draft submissions of a similar quality?

Initially, Robin thought it was always going to be quicker to do it himself. But drafting good submissions was something that other people ought to be trained to do. What he was ideally equipped to contribute was his understanding of what would or would not work with ministers. He developed the skill of steering and mentoring others, where the distinctiveness he brought was about understanding the likely reaction of ministers, because he had more access to ministers than did his staff.

Eileen was chief executive of an agency and loved her work. She was far too busy and knew that she had to use her time and energy more selectively. She asked herself, where can I add value? But in most of what she did she was adding value. When she changed the question to "What is it only I can do?" the list became shorter. Much of what she did could be done by others, even if not quite to the same high standards she would apply.

What only Eileen could do as a leader was about setting a clear vision, deciding on financial allocations, ensuring the right relationship with the chair, ensuring that key stakeholders were understood and responded to effectively. She recognised that the tone she set was just as important as the decisions she made. People in the organisation would mirror her approach and demeanour. If she came across as calm, clear-headed and controlled, then there was a likelihood that her approach would be mirrored across the organisation.

Jack held a senior position within a police force. When a major incident occurred he got his deputy to lead on the operational issues. He saw his job as interfacing with the politicians and the media. He put his credibility on the line and focused externally so that his deputy was not disturbed in dealing with the operational issues. Because of his rank and experience, his distinctive contribution was outward-looking.

When the income figures for a consulting organisation were beginning to dip the chief executive knew she had to take responsibility with the shareholders. The finance director and the operations director were fully prepared to stand up and be counted and take responsibility, but the chief executive knew that in order to calm the shareholders she had to be unwavering in taking the lead and demonstrating that corrective action was being taken. This was not an occasion to put a number two in the limelight. Just as she took the glory when business was going well, she had to take the rap when profits were likely to dip.

The answer to the question, "What is it only I can do?" will vary in different contexts and times. Sometimes it might be providing a clear and distinctive lead. On other occasions it might involve staying calm, reassuring people and saying now is not the moment to change. In both instances, what is needed is a sense of independence and detachment so that the leader is making their own decisions and is not captive to the views and expectations of others.

WHAT IS IT ONLY YOU CAN DO?

- What is brought together at your level?
- Who can you influence more effectively than others?
- What accountabilities do you have that others do not have?
- What is it you can do that affects uniquely the viability of an enterprise?
- If you were not around what would not happen?
- What will members of the team get from you that they would not get from other people?
- What unique insights does your background and experience bring?
- What distinctive contribution do other people expect you to offer?
- What, intuitively, do you feel is the most distinctive contribution you can make?
- How best can you complement and add to others' contributions?
- Are there roles that only you can fill?

POINTS FOR REFLECTION

- Where could you focus your contribution even more?
- What are the two or three contributions that only you can make?
- Can you accept more readily that the key question is not where do you add value, but what is it only you can do?
- How best do you bring people on board as you focus more on what only you can do?

Chapter 23

WHERE DO YOUR FAMILY AND FRIENDS FIT IN?

Margaret was preoccupied with getting the balance right at work between her own and her colleagues' contributions. Life revolved around her work. When she was not focused on a particular task, she was thinking about how she could work more effectively with her colleagues and her team.

Margaret was not desperately ambitious for promotion, but she wanted to make a significant difference in her position within local government. She accepted that the pressure was relentless and there was always more to be done and limited resources at her disposal.

Margaret was single and content to be independent. There had been boyfriends in the past but intellectually they had never been her equal and she had become bored with them. Margaret doted on her godson and fully recognised the depth of pleasure she got out of the time spent with him. There were three or four good girlfriends with whom she could joke and share a bottle of wine, but nobody got very close to Margaret.

Margaret was hugely trusted within the local authority. The politicians would phone her for reassurance at any time of day. Margaret liked this sense of being indispensable. She admitted she was a workaholic because her work gave her immense satisfaction. Some friends tried to encourage Margaret to take more time off work and to take up other interests. Margaret laughed and thanked them for their interest. Margaret had found her own equilibrium and that was fine for her. She regularly worked more than 60 hours a week but was fine with that. Her godson and her core group of friends were devoted to her. Margaret knew that when she did need the intimacy of close friendship, it was available.

For Rita the equilibrium was less straightforward. She was very ambitious and energetic but knew that periodically she would exhaust herself, become indecisive and have to rest for a few days. This cycle had started at university and had been part of her working life for 20 years. Sometimes she enjoyed this relentless cycle, while on other occasions, she felt trapped. Rita's marriage had not lasted long and she now shared her home with Joanne, her female companion. Joanne was calmer and more domesticated. She enjoyed Rita's energy and was happy to be nursemaid when Rita exhausted herself. Theirs was a compatible and supportive friendship. They drew strength and encouragement from each other and accepted each other's failings just as much as enjoying their qualities.

John was a senior executive with responsibility for 1,000 people. For half a day most weekends he would go cycling with a group of guys. He never talked about his working life when in the company of the cyclists. All they knew was that he worked in an office. His fellow cyclists talked about their lives as policemen, firemen and factory workers. He enjoyed their company immensely. They took him into a different world that was full of physical endeavour and blokeish camaraderie. He treasured their friendship because it was entirely unrelated to his work. The only difficult moment was when one of them saw his photograph in the newspaper after he had been awarded a special honour. Thankfully, by then his friends knew him as a good mate and saw his senior leadership role as an irrelevance.

The point of these stories is to illustrate the importance of finding equilibrium with family and friends that works for you. For many, the support network follows the traditional pattern of spouse, close family and good, long-term friends. But the right equilibrium for you might appear unorthodox to others. We all need trusted others with whom we can share our successes and open up about our concerns. As human beings we need the companionship of others, recognising the primary richness that friendship provides in one particular dimension of our lives. Often that friendship comes where there is collective endeavour, be it on the sports field, in a community activity, in a religious community or in a professional association.

For many people the ideal may be the intimacy of some close family relationships and friendships that transcend a range of interests, alongside more limited and focused friendships and collaborations that follow from shared work, activities and hobbies.

WHERE DO YOUR FAMILY AND FRIENDS FIT IN?

- Who in your family gives you energy?
- Who are the friends who enable you to work through the most difficult problems to a satisfactory conclusion?
- Which members of your family might you invest more time in?
- Who among your family and friends has been particularly supportive and how might you repay that support?
- Which friendships should you nurture because they are creative and enabling?
- With whom can we share a valued focus on mutual mentoring that enables each of us to be more effective in our work and make a fuller contribution within our family?

POINTS FOR REFLECTION

- What practical steps would you like to take to build a stronger sense of partnership with members of your family?
- Which friendships in different spheres of your life might you want to invest in so there is a stronger sense of shared endeavour?
- How would you like to rebalance between your individual aspirations and those of family members and friends you are close to?

Chapter 24
WHEN DOES THE TEAM COME FIRST?

The long-distance cyclist is very dependant upon colleagues in their team. They take it in turn to lead the group. They pace their use of energy to complement the needs and preferences of other members of the team. Personal performance is important but the individual cyclist excels when the team is working well.

The church is decked with flowers for a wedding when all those preparing the flower arrangements have completed their tasks. It would look very odd if the wedding began and two people were still arranging the flowers in one of the windows. The job of the team is only completed when the last window has been decked with flowers.

When a festrift is being written for a retiring professor with contributions from a range of people, the book can only be finalised and published when every contribution has been received. Editing a book with a range of contributors is like leading a convoy that can only go at the speed of the slowest ship.

When famous rugby players retire from international competition, they often suffer an inner turmoil. Ideally, the player wants to keep competing at international level, but he accepts that the team might be better off without him, with younger players taking his role. Rather than trying to maintain a place based on past loyalties, the rugby player concludes that now is the time to retire with honour and fully support the team in its next phase.

You are an energetic member of your department with a good relationship with the head of department. Your peers are not held in such high esteem. Is it in your interest to keep differentiating your performance as better than those around you, or is it better to raise the performance of the whole department so that your colleagues are also seen as performing well? The cynic in you might prefer the first option, but in the long run the second approach is likely to be more consistent with your values and also suit your long-term interests.

The individual who is supportive of others and able to help them develop is more likely to be seen as a potential long-term leader. The individual who enables their colleague to excel and ensures that the team succeeds may sometimes feel that their contribution goes unnoticed. But an individual who can be a source of encouragement and enable a range of people to progress is likely to become regarded as a key team member. The risk is that you can become too indispensable in an individual role and not promoted as quickly as you would like. But that might be a short-term disbenefit rather than long-term disaster.

Good teams are more than the sum of their parts. Participants bring the best out in each other and enable creative and bold solutions to be devised to address previously intractable problems. Putting the interest of the team first can result in stimulating, exciting interaction that pushes the boundaries of previous thinking, bringing forth shared solutions.

Some of the most creative conversations I was involved in were as a board member of the newly formed Department for Education and Skills, as we worked on a set of values and behaviours for the new organisation. We were a mix of people from very different backgrounds, and the conclusions we arrived at as a group were far better than we would have achieved as individuals. This was creative dialogue at its best. Over ten years later, I still carry around in my top pocket a card with those agreed values printed on it.

Sometimes, putting the team first can mean subjugating our individual interest. This does not mean agreeing with the views of others at any cost. It means being clear about your fixed points and where you want to find a strong sense of shared agreement, so that the combined energy and commitment of the team is far more than that of the individuals within it.

WHEN DOES THE TEAM COME FIRST?

- When a successful outcome depends on the performance of the whole team and not of individuals.
- When the team working together can have a bigger effect than individuals operating alone.
- When an individual does not have some of the skills and perspectives that are brought by other members of the team.
- When your interests have moved on and it is right for your sake, and that of the team, that there is a new beginning.
- When the next phase for the project is better suited to other participants than you.
- When you are not fully effective because of illness, injury or distraction.
- When you know that your support of colleagues can ensure the team's success, even if your own immediate contribution is more limited.

POINTS FOR REFLECTION

- How might you enhance the effectiveness of groups or teams you are part of?
- How might you pull back so others can grow?
- How bold do you want to be in stretching others and enabling the team to do well?

DIRECTIVE AND RESPONSIVE

This section looks at the balance between being directive and responsive. If we are always directive we end up exhausting ourselves, and everyone around us. If we are always responsive, we are likely to become known as lacking initiative and unable to take a lead.

Getting the balance right between being directive and responsive requires an ability to read a situation well and to have a good sense of timing. It is linked to an understanding of how decisions are made that individuals and groups accept and readily take forward. The success of a leader or manager comes from the capacity to be both directive and responsive in a way that is true to your own values and philosophy, while carrying people with you so you are not isolated or ignored.

This chapter examines: when do you take control; when do you go with the flow; who are you captive to; and can you build a virtuous circle of being both responsive and directive?

Chapter 25
WHEN DO YOU TAKE CONTROL?

There is a task to be done and you see a clear way forward. You have a responsibility to ensure action happens. You can take control and begin to tell people what to do. It feels to you like a military operation where you are enjoying the responsibility. People keep asking you questions and you are revelling in this newfound authority.

There are moments when it is right to take control. After a road accident or other emergency someone needs to make decisions and tell people what to do. In any crisis when urgent action is necessary, someone needs to take action and say what needs to be done.

Taking control is not about random shouting out of instructions. It is about using experience and credibility well, and then ensuring a coherent set of next steps that can be explained after the event. In a sports game the captain has to make quick decisions. There has to be enough trust that the captain will make the right decision, or at least the best one on the basis of available evidence. The good team captain will explain after a match why they took a sequence of decisions rather than leave people wondering why some moves had been used and not others.

The parent with a young child has to take control of the environment in which the toddler is operating. Bottom shelves are cleared and precious objects are placed higher up. The parent who does not take control is not acting responsibly. The toddler who knocked over a precious piece of glass and cut their hand is not acting irresponsibly: it is the parent who failed to take control of the environment and left the fragile piece of glass accessible to the toddler.

As a facilitator working with groups of adults I have to take control of a master class. But I do not achieve this by telling people what to do or think. It is my job to create an environment where there is trust and openness so that participants feel confident sharing ideas, talking with each other and building actions for the future. It is my task to create a controlled environment so that individuals can crystallize their own thinking and next steps.

Wendy led a group of architects who were creative, independently minded people. Being team leader of this group felt like "herding cats". The last thing Wendy wanted to do was suppress their individuality and creativity, but there needed to be discipline in how work was allocated and clear expectations about what was delivered and to what timescale. Wendy did not want to control their creativity, but she did want to bring a degree of control about how they managed their time and energy. She introduced peer review across the team. She balanced her focus on meeting timescales alongside a big push on sharing creative ideas. Wendy felt she had got the balance about right, but she knew that the architects needed to accept and deliver on her expectations about meeting timescales and the quality of work.

Jack was responsible for a production line in a factory. A strong measure of control was essential so that all the products met tough quality standards. The tolerance for failure was minimal, but he could not control every individual action. He built a culture where quality control was accepted by everyone as essential, with a tight control over every step in the production line being recognised as necessary. However, this highly disciplined approach was counterbalanced by the high energy of the factory sports teams, which bordered on the overzealous – but perhaps this was a natural reaction to the discipline of the production line.

WHEN DO YOU TAKE CONTROL?

- There is an emergency and action is needed quickly.
- You have a particular expertise and credibility that no one else has.
- You have the ultimate authority and are expected to make decisions.
- You have a responsibility that others accept is yours and yours alone.
- No one else is willing to take control when it is essential that a decision is made.
- The responsibility to make decisions is yours for a period and then passes to someone else.
- If you do not take control there is a risk in terms of the health and safety of others.

POINTS FOR REFLECTION

- In what situations would you naturally take control?
- How hesitant are you about taking control?
- What approval or support do you need from others to be comfortable taking control?

Can you think of a current situation where you need to take control and ensure action is taken?

- What is holding you back?
- What might prompt you into action?
- What would be the benefits of you taking control?
- How do you best handle those who might have reservations about you taking control?

Chapter 26
WHEN DO YOU GO WITH THE FLOW?

If you are coming down a ski slope there are risks in trying to brake abruptly. You need to "go with the flow" down the slope rather than jerking to an ungainly halt. When cycling with a friend who is willing to cycle at the front, you can enjoy being in their slipstream and not having to expend so much energy.

Going with the flow can sometimes feel like a cop out. It can feel like going along with the crowd and not putting your own stamp on what is happening. But sometimes going with the flow is the most effective and enjoyable step to take. If you are enjoying a comedy TV programme, you settle down into your chair and relish the ridiculous or enjoy the light-hearted jokes. In this case, going with the flow lifts your spirits. There is no point in fighting it or thinking that you could tell better jokes!

When elected leaders have made decisions, going with the flow is generally the right thing to do. If a government has a mandate for action in a particular area, there is a good case to use our individual energy to ensure effective implementation of agreed policies.

There are times when it is right to "stand against the tide". Sometimes a stand is needed, but going against the flow rarely works when the action is haphazard or ill thought through. Standing up to the flow will always require clear argument, good evidence, strong partnership and personal resilience.

Richard was convinced that the organisation had made a poor decision about an IT solution it intended to adopt. He had argued against this solution but recognised he was in a minority. He chose to go with the flow and do his level best to ensure the preparatory work went well so that the solution could be implemented effectively. He continued to have reservations about the solution and explored different alternatives.

When two or three other people began to express serious reservations he knew this was the right moment to make his concerns known and seek a formal review. In the end, his preferred solution was chosen. He reflected that it had been right to go with the flow for a period because he would not have been successful if he had pressed the alternative case too early. Success came through listening to other people's views and then choosing the moment to argue his viewpoint as part of a shared set of concerns.

Michael worked as a train guard for a railway company. He always maintained an informal and friendly approach, even when the passengers became edgy with him. If a train was delayed, he would provide as much information as possible and be sympathetic to the personal circumstances of travellers. He would "go with the flow" of their concerns and frustrations while making sure that they knew that action was in hand to correct the problem and enable the train to reach its destination in reasonable time. He did not control the signalling on the railway line. His success as a train guard was recognising the emotions of his passengers and engaging with them as fellow travellers, rather than treating them as the "bad tempered and indignant of Surrey".

Going with the flow may sometimes seem like a "cop out". But often there is no alternative or it is better to bide one's time.

WHEN DO YOU GO WITH THE FLOW?

- When you think the action embarked upon is right.
- When you believe that those taking the action have the wisdom, experience and credibility to be doing the right thing.
- When action is more important than discussion.
- When your time and energy is focused on other things and you are happy to accept the judgement of others.
- When others are more concerned about a particular activity than you are, and the outcome is of less importance to you.
- When you know others are focusing on the right next steps, even though your emotional preferences are different.
- When failing to go with the flow is dangerous for you personally.

WHEN DO YOU NOT GO WITH THE FLOW?

- When the proposed action is destructive.
- When there are moral principles at stake that are important to you.
- When the action proposed is inconsistent with your values.
- When you making a stand will encourage others to do the same.
- When you are willing to sacrifice some of your personal reputation for the greater good.
- When you would be unable to live with your conscience if you failed to stand up and be counted.

POINTS FOR REFLECTION

- Can you reflect on a couple of current situations where in one case you are going with the flow and in another you are standing against the flow?
- What is different about these two situations that has led to your contrasting stances?

In what situations are you likely to:
- Regularly go with the flow.
- Want to think very carefully before going with the flow.
- Be clear that you intend to speak out against the majority perspective.

Chapter 27
WHO ARE YOU CAPTIVE TO?

We all have heroes. The people we admire inevitably have a big impact on us. As we enter new and demanding situations we might reflect on how our heroes would deal with the expectations and pressures.

Role models provide an inspiration that can enable us to raise our game and achieve far more than we might originally have anticipated. As a young boy brought up in Yorkshire by a widowed mother, two powerful sources of inspiration for me were a teacher at school and the leader of a local youth group. They helped me set my sights towards university and a life beyond a small Yorkshire town. Perhaps we do not celebrate enough those individuals in our past who have been role models and have been sources of inspiration to us.

But can we sometimes be captive to those individuals who have inspired us? Is there a risk that we mimic their approach and believe that if we behave as they did, then all will be well? Sometimes we may be unsure about our own capabilities, and consequently revert to imitating the approach of someone we admire. Admiration can become a form of captivity.

How can we adopt the best from others and at the same time be true to ourselves and the strength within us? Embracing what we admire from a range of different people rather than one or two particular heroes can help. Trying to understand the journey that an individual we admire has been on can help in following our own path, rather than taking on someone else's set of attitudes as a "job lot". Understanding what has shaped those we admire can enable us to appreciate how we have been shaped by our experience and identify the distinctive strengths within us.

We may feel captive to our boss. We want to do their bidding, and have their approval to ensure we have a good performance assessment. We want to be praised and not criticised by our boss but can we fall into a "yes sir" mentality too easily?

When I was a senior civil servant I was expected to do whatever the ministers of the day wanted. I was under their authority and paid to implement the policies of the elected government. But if I just slavishly implemented their every whim I would not have been doing my job properly. My role as a senior civil servant was to implement their policies, but it was also my responsibility to bring out relevant facts and perspectives to enable a minister to work through different options and to see the implications of different choices. My task was to understand the ministers' objectives and work with them to find the most effective solutions. The best relationships I had with ministers were close partnerships based on mutual respect, and not captivity to their whims.

The most productive relationship with a boss is where there is a clear understanding of where the boss is coming from, combined with an openness of communication that allows the merits of different options to be expressed openly and constructively. A good working relationship involves no sense of captivity or captivation, but is both cordial and constructive.

Jane had a strong feeling that her boss, Bill, wanted her to do precisely what he asked down to the last detail. This pressure made Jane feel edgy and sometimes fearful. Jane felt as if she was in a cage, captured by Bill, with no chance of breaking out of a very structured regime. On Monday mornings Jane was reluctant to go into work. She concluded that she had to talk through her reactions with Bill. Bill was far more receptive than she expected and apologised for his restrictive approach. Jane now understood more where Bill was coming from. Bill began to give her more freedom and Jane had the confidence to press for greater discretion. Jane felt much less captive, with a greater freedom to take the initiative.

WHAT OR WHO MIGHT YOU BE CAPTIVE TO?

- Those you admire from the past?
- Your boss or your sense of what the boss wants?
- Your beliefs about other people's expectations of you?
- Your own expectations about yourself?
- A particular view of success that comes from your culture or faith?
- A historical self-image that is now out of date?
- A conflicting set of priorities within yourself?

POINTS FOR REFLECTION

- Who might you be captive to in the future?
- What are the approaches you might adopt to break out of this captivity?

POSSIBLE APPROACHES MIGHT INCLUDE:

- Be amused by the way you hang on to previous images of yourself and others.
- Allow yourself to see the ridiculous in the way you are captured by others.
- How might you both embrace the best in others and put your own stamp on the attitudes and approaches you intend to adopt from now on?

Chapter 28

CAN YOU BUILD A VIRTUOUS CIRCLE OF BEING RESPONSIVE AND DIRECTIVE?

The best working relationships are both directive and responsive. When I was a director general in government there was one deputy director who worked for me when I was in three roles. Carol upwardly managed me brilliantly. She could be very direct with me when she thought I was on the wrong track. But Carol was also completely responsive when she accepted that the direction that I thought was right was appropriate. There was a quality of dialogue between us that meant we could both be directive and responsive with each other. When we worked on big finance issues I knew that she would push back if she thought I was wrong: this greatly helped me develop different ideas and approaches, knowing that they would be objectively assessed.

Being directive and responsive are in some ways two sides of the same coin. There is no point in being directive unless you understand how people are going to respond. If your directions are ignored or taken forward in a half-hearted way then there is little point in making a firm statement of intent. The good leader has to understand how people are likely to respond before there is any point in being directive.

The foreman who insists that a particular building project is going to be completed by the end of the month needs to understand the attitude and approach of his workforce to know what will motivate and incentivise them to complete the work on time. Words alone will rarely deliver the desired outcome.

The time to be directive may be when the task is clear, the timetable is immovable, the risks are obvious and roles are explicit. The time to be more responsive may be when there is on-going debate about key issues, attitudes are still changing, key facts have yet to be established and there is a degree of flexibility in the timetable.

The best run projects combine being responsive with being directive. There is dialogue about the next phase with a set of conclusions about what needs to be delivered over the forthcoming months and a set of agreed actions to implement those objectives. As that phase nears completion, there is another cycle of responsive debate and then clarity about the directive action needed. Effective teams often use a combination of individuals who are completer/finishers and others who are reflectors. In the most effective teams the roles can switch between individuals over time.

Derek worked for a cruise liner with responsibility for customer service. Derek had to be directive in setting out clear standards about what would be delivered for customers. On the other hand he had to be responsive to the views of different groups of customers. Yes, "the customer is king", and he always wanted to be responsive. But there were times when the customer would ask for things that were too expensive, or would have implications for other customers or would set an unhelpful precedent. Sometimes Derek had to say, "no".

Derek knew from experience that how he said "No" was crucial. It was often a matter of being responsive to the customers' emotions and trying to find a solution to their concerns without necessarily giving them precisely what they wanted. He knew that if he was regarded as a push-over, expectations from customers would get higher and higher and his credibility within the business could be tarnished. Derek had to be both responsive to his boss and to the customers, and find a way that satisfied both. Sometimes he had to be directive to ensure that unhelpful practices were changed. Derek had to keep his bosses and his customers content by a judicious combination of being directive and responsive.

HOW BEST DO YOU BUILD A VIRTUOUS CIRCLE OF BEING RESPONSIVE AND DIRECTIVE?

- What is important to be directive about and what can be left to take its own course?
- How do you build an acceptance of the need to be directive?
- How do you demonstrate responsiveness in order to build an acceptance that you can be directive?
- How do you ensure that when you are responsive it comes over as a sign of strength and not weakness?
- How do you create working relationships that are both directive and responsive?
- Who will give you accurate feedback about whether you have got this balance right?

POINTS FOR REFLECTION

- As you reflect on your own leadership approach over the next few weeks, are there examples where you are too directive or too responsive?
- Are there situations where you need to modify the balance between being directive and being responsive?
- How might you take forward the idea of creating a virtuous circle of being responsive and directive in both a work context and in activities outside work?

REALISM AND OPTIMISM

Finding a balance between realism and optimism is one of the most important tasks of a manager. We need to be both rooted in reality and see the potential for change in the future. Without realism we are captive to wishful thinking. Without a sense of optimism we are ground down by current reality. We need realism to keep us grounded, and optimism to keep us uplifted.

But optimism that is pure fantasy is delusion. Realism that only sees the dark side will send us into inner turmoil and dejection. This section reinforces the importance of a rootedness that is adaptable and an optimism that is grounded. It explores accepting harsh reality, believing that hope springs eternal, acknowledging that there is always a silver lining and being able to deal with apparent contradictions.

Chapter 29
ACCEPTING HARSH REALITY

Sometimes we have to accept harsh reality and move on. The company has gone bankrupt, the organisation has been taken over, the project has been cancelled or the business has collapsed because the market has changed. When these things occur we have no option but to accept it. That's life.

When harsh reality hits we go through a grieving process. We are angry, feel abused, want to get our own back, are depressed and want to "kick the cat" and anything else that happens to be in the way. Grieving about harsh reality is inevitable and necessary. It does not take the pain away, but it enables us to live through it and come out the other side.

The easy thing to say to someone going through these experiences is that it was inevitable, or is probably a good thing, or you will later come to see it as a positive, not a negative, life-changing moment. But such comments can appear trite and unhelpful. When someone is going through a harsh reality the most supportive contribution is just to be there and listen and not try to be too "bouncy" in response.

Facing harsh reality can be painful. The hard work and effort of many years can feel devalued. Your pride is hurt and your contribution can feel as nothing. You regret all the energy that you committed to a particular endeavour now it is ending in apparent failure. Your emotions are in a whirl and you feel physically sick. You can feel intellectually abused. You can feel spiritually as if

God has knocked you back for no reason. Accepting harsh reality is about accepting these emotional, physical, intellectual and spiritual reactions, sitting with them and letting them gradually dissipate and move on.

Sometimes it is right to fight back. When a wrong has been done you want to correct it. But if the organisation has been taken over you are not going to stop it happening. If the company has gone bankrupt you are not going to single-handedly turn the finances of the organisation around. You feel stuck in the trenches with bombs exploding around you. There is absolutely nothing you can do other than sit and wait for the explosions to subside and resist the temptation to do anything foolhardy.

Time does heal and the grief cycle has to work itself through. The devastation you feel when your organisation closes or is taken over will subside, even if you feel that bad decisions have been taken. You fail to get a promotion and feel hard done by. You will feel aggrieved, but gradually you may accept that the timing was not right, or someone else is better suited, or you needed to have prepared in a different way.

Joel was the finance director of a government agency. Unexpectedly, the government decided to combine two agencies. Joel threw himself into the work of building the best possible newly combined agency. He enjoyed the challenge and the opportunity to think in fresh ways. It suddenly dawned on him that the new agency would have only one finance director and that the two existing finance directors would be competing for the post. This realisation did not stop him working hard to ensure the new agency was set up effectively.

Joel came second in the competition to be appointed the new finance director. He accepted, intellectually, that the chosen candidate was better suited, but emotionally he thought he could have done the job just as well, that his efforts had been wasted and that his future employment opportunities would be damaged. Joel kept hearing encouraging words from colleagues that washed over him. He knew that he had to accept that there was some damage to his prospects, and that he needed to present his credentials in a different way. What mattered to Joel in these difficult days was the sense that there were people around him who believed in him. It was their emotional support rather than their words that were important to him.

WAYS OF ACCEPTING HARSH REALITY

· Recognise that harsh reality hits everyone.
· Reflect on a harsh reality you have faced before and how you have come through it.
· Be objective about the inevitability of being faced with a harsh reality.
· See a harsh reality as not as bad as it might have been.
· Accept that there is a grieving process as you go through a harsh reality.
· Accept your emotional, physical, intellectual and spiritual reactions and don't expect them to change overnight.
· Listen to expressions of emotional support from others.
· Do other activities that are completely disconnected with the harsh reality.
· Do some physically demanding activity that energises you and tires you out.

POINTS FOR REFLECTION

· What types of harsh reality are you now having to live with?
· Where are you currently on the grieving cycle?
· What other harsh reality might you need to prepare for?
· What are the patterns you, personally, go through when harsh reality hits?

Chapter 30
HOPE SPRINGS ETERNAL

Surviving and thriving depend on dreaming dreams that are rooted in reality, our values and our aspirations. Whatever the reality of the situation, if we believe that individuals can change, that dysfunctional organisations can be renewed, that broken relationships can be healed, that individuals can raise their game beyond expectations, that out of apparent failure there can be new beginnings – then our dreams have the potential of becoming true.

Dreams are not about wishful thinking. They include reflection beyond our current expectations or frames of reference. They are about allowing ourselves to be bold and courageous in seeking to create purposeful aspirations and more creative and supportive teams and groupings in the workplace and beyond.

We can dismiss our hopes and aspirations as mere dreams and false optimism, but perhaps these dreams can provide us with a new future reality. When we are rooted in our values, have a clear vision about what we want to contribute, allow ourselves to bring a value-added contribution that brings out the best in us, appreciate anew the sources of our vitality – then we can make a difference that far exceeds our expectations.

Surviving and thriving is about living with the dual realities of both our work context and what is going on in our hearts and minds, and keeping the two in equilibrium. Thriving is not about linear progression. There will be moments when our efforts seem irrelevant, our contribution dismissed and the future unclear.

What can keep us positive is seeing beyond the immediate focus to a key change we want to make happen going forward, and to an adventure we want to embark upon in our thinking or approach.

Sitting back and dreaming dreams is not a waste of time. It was not a waste for Martin Luther King. Allowing ourselves to dream can create new hopes and aspirations. Of course, they need to be tested against reality. But with a blank page we can sometimes imagine solutions or approaches that we have not thought of before. We can be surprised by our own sense of creativity. And then we may need to be careful what we wish for because it might come true....

In 2003 I had to accept the harsh reality that my current job was coming to an end. It was not an easy time as I went through a grieving process. I tried various options but the doors were closed. But I loved mentoring and coaching people. I dreamed of turning that activity into a full-time role. The dream both motivated me and helped to create an objective worth striving for. From the harsh reality emerged a sense of hope that good could come out of this. The result has been nearly 10 years of working with individuals and groups across five continents. The harsh reality turned into a dream that is still unfolding.

Barbara went into banking after leaving university. Initially she enjoyed her career but gradually became more and more fed up. She was not inspired by the work and felt that she had sold her soul to a financial institution that was not really interested in her. Her passion was enabling children to grow and develop. She loved her work with a group of 8–10 year olds at junior church.

Barbara was challenged by her friends, who asked her about her dream. If she hated banking what was she going to do about it? Barbara needed to be both encouraged and cajoled. Barbara toyed with the idea of being a teacher and visited a couple of primary schools to observe. She felt energised. The dream was taking shape.

Barbara gave in her resignation and felt liberated. She spent time as a trainee teacher and loved it: the dream was coming true.

Within four years she was a deputy head and within another three years she was the head of a primary school. Looking back, Barbara was so relieved that she had allowed herself to dream dreams, and taken the risk of moving into a new sphere. She trusted the hope and passion within her, lived the dream and relished all that subsequently happened. She was a far better head teacher because she had been through the harsh reality of a first career that did not work for her.

In tough times what is the hope within you? Hope springs eternal – there is always a desire to bounce back, move on and dream dreams that will help us survive and thrive.

CAPTURING THE HOPE WITHIN YOU

- What were your dreams in earlier days?
- If you were 21 again, what would you like to do?
- What seems like an impossible dream that might inspire you?
- What do other people who know you well say to you about your qualities and where you could make a difference?
- In what areas of your life could you allow yourself to start afresh and dream dreams?
- Who are the people you can talk to openly about the type of next steps that you would like to take? Which of them are likely to inspire and motivate you?

POINTS FOR REFLECTION

- Is there a current dream that would be good to think through and decide whether you can take it forward?
- What sort of physical space would enable the hope within you to come to the fore? It might involve going for a long walk or a swim or sitting by the sea.
- What dreams would you like to nurture in others that will encourage you to take your dreams forward?
- How might you believe more fully that "hope springs eternal" and that past limitations may not be as restrictive as you had previously thought?

Chapter 31
THERE IS ALWAYS A SILVER LINING

Whatever the issue or crisis, there will almost inevitably be a silver lining to the cloud. An often-used phrase is, "Never waste a good crisis". When Robin Hindle-Fisher and I wrote the booklet, *Seizing the Future* (Praesta, 2010), we drew on observations from leaders in a range of different organisations. It was clear that *Seizing the Future* demanded an upbeat and assertive approach coupled with realism, humility and the confidence to lead by example. It involved standing back, re-evaluating and being liberated from constraining frames of reference.

A key theme from conversations with leaders was the importance of accepting a new reality. We identified three important steps:

- Accept that conditions have changed and let go of the past as a first step towards making the most of future opportunities. Embracing this new reality might begin by recognising that the past has gone and adjusting emotionally to what has been "lost". It means standing back and seeing the journey to date and working out how to deal with obstacles that are now in the way.

- Calibrate the gap between the old and the new so you are ruthlessly honest about where you are now and the degree of challenge ahead. It can involve acknowledging that parts of your organisation are in trouble, with no clear view of the way forward. The new reality may be more demanding and require focusing on new outcomes.

- Allow yourself to feel a touch of excitement amidst the new landscape. You may feel daunted or dejected, but the new reality can include new opportunities if you adjust your perspective.

Leaders and managers who have been through demanding times will almost always acknowledge there were new opportunities created by the change. The belief that opportunities will always be there is important to hold on to. You do have to focus on where they are likely to be and, in some circumstances, get ahead of the competition. Fewer resources forces difficult questions to be asked. Those who bring insight and perspective and can spot trends and discontinuities will be in a strong position to innovate and may receive a more receptive audience than ever before.

Crises and the need for quick action often throw into question whether existing practices are right. After the looting riots in London in August 2011 the Tribunals and Courts Service responded adroitly in arranging court times that went through the night in order to ensure the legal proceedings took place quickly. This demonstrated that the traditional pattern of court opening hours was not inviolate, which led to fresh thinking about how best to use the time of the courts.

For decades, the resources available to the National Health Service in the UK increased significantly each year. As resources have become much tighter in recent years, it has meant that questions have been asked in a more rigorous way about how best resources are used and which restrictive practices need to be changed. The result has been a step change, with a more efficient use of resources and much more flexibility in the way staff time is employed.

Out of disaster has come major reform. The plight of soldiers in World War I led to major medical advances. Aircraft crashes have led to a much clearer understanding of aircraft safety. Nuclear power disasters have led to a much better grasp of nuclear safety. No one would have wished these disasters to happen. But out of these tragic events has come a passion by individuals to make a difference and improve wellbeing for the next generation.

The school examination system in England and Wales had been unchanged for many years up until 2000. In 2002 there was a major problem about the calibration of Advanced ('A') Level results. The silver lining to this big cloud was the opportunity it gave for reform of the 14–18 examination system. There was a moment in time when major change could have happened. In the event, the government of the day decided to draw back from major change and the opportunity passed.

This example illustrates the importance of both looking for the silver lining in any cloud and when you see the opportunity, seizing the moment. Once the moment has gone it might have disappeared forever.

LOOKING FOR THE SILVER LINING

- Always believe that good can come out of any situation.
- Keep a look out for an opportunity to make a difference in any new reality.
- Never believe that every crisis is all about bad news.
- Allow yourself a touch of excitement about where changes might lead.
- Always believe that you can find a new purpose and passion, whatever the harsh reality of the current situation.

POINTS FOR REFLECTION

- Can you think of a crisis or difficult period in the past where there was a silver lining?
- What might a crisis or difficult period you are currently going through liberate you from?
- Looking forward, what type of silver lining can you detect forming?
- How can you ensure that you avoid falling into a pit of despair, where you believe that every silver lining is a mirage?

Chapter 32

DEALING WITH APPARENT CONTRADICTIONS

Can you be rooted in realism and optimistic at the same time, or is this double talk or self-delusion? The initial evidence might point in one direction. But where you have a hope and belief that you can create an impetus for change, then holding on to your belief for as long as you can is important. The mountaineer might know all the reasons why they are not going to be able to climb the mountain, but sheer, dogged endurance gets them to the top. The belief that the summit can be reached has meant that many individuals have achieved far more than they ever thought possible. They have been sustained by a sense of hope or optimism rooted in their own personal beliefs and values.

We all live with contradictions in ourselves. We know we are good at some things and less surefooted at others. We are aware that some people bring out the best in others while other people bring out the worst. We are rarely models of consistency. Our emotions take us to heights of achievement or depths of despair. We can sometimes feel like we are on a rollercoaster as we live with the apparent contradictions in our actions, attitudes and emotions.

The more we know ourselves the more we are able to live with our contradictions and use them to positive effect: we know that one day we see grey as nearly black and on another day will see the same grey as closer to white. The more we understand the patterns in ourselves, the more we are able to live with the contradictions in others and in the situations we are in.

Andrew worked in an architectural consultancy where the rhetoric was all about growth and the vision all about creating a successful, international organisation. The message from the leadership was optimistic with a focus on "ever upwards". However, the reality was that the market was falling and the company's market share was going down. The organisation had debts that were accumulating and the banks were demanding higher interest payments.

Andrew recognised that he had to communicate a positive view of the future with his people, but he was determined to keep his sense of realism. He worked hard on developing work with clients in sectors that were less impacted by the recession. When talking with his people he tried to balance realism with a positive view of what they were seeking to achieve while being honest about the risks and uncertainties ahead. It was a delicate balancing act in which being honest with himself was vital. He was open with his people about the company's vision for the future and the reality of the situation, but decided not to share his darkest fears.

A sense of optimism rooted in reality is essential for any organisation to grow and thrive. A church that has a declining membership has to maintain a belief that they can have an impact for good on the community around. If there is no passion to have an impact, then the decline will become terminal. In circumstances where numbers are declining, the church needs to decide on what areas it wishes to focus and how it wants to ensure that it continues to make an impact in its community.

Good leadership is about making a virtue of the inevitability that an organisation cannot deliver in every area it wants. It has to be realistic and "cut its coat to suit its cloth". But keeping a vision and a sense of optimism is vital for survival, even if the focus of that optimism is narrowed to a particular area.

DEALING WITH APPARENT CONTRADICTIONS

- Be honest with yourself about the contradictions.
- Recognise how you have successfully handled contradictions in the past.
- Talk through with trusted others the contradictions you are living with.
- Focus your optimism so that it is compatible with a realistic assessment of the resources available.
- Believe that sometimes contradictions just have to be lived with.
- Take satisfaction in stopping doing certain things, or stopping believing certain things can happen, where previous optimism turned out to be foolhardy.
- Look for sources of grounded optimism in every situation.

POINTS FOR REFLECTION

- What contradictions are you currently living with and how successfully are you coping with them?
- What contradictions are you finding difficult to live with and what steps can you take to make them more manageable?
- In what areas do you need to trim your optimism and have more realistic expectations?
- Which contradictions do you now need to understand and fix?

CONTINUITY AND CHANGE

"Continuity and Change" has been the title of at least one UK Government White Paper. The phrase flows easily off the tongue. Achieving both continuity and change sounds as if it might be straightforward, but it is rarely that easy. In any organisation, what one person wants to change is often a core part of continuity for another person. An organisation which links continuity and change together is often using it as a banner for either presenting a unified front when there is plenty of disagreement below the surface, or is trying to persuade the sceptics of action when nothing is actually going to change.

Doing continuity and change will lead to very different responses in different situations. It is almost certainly not going to be an easy ride. This section looks at different aspects of continuity and change, namely: keeping straight on to the end of the road; it is an upside down world; being willing to turn sideways; and three steps forward and two steps back. This is a rollercoaster section where markedly different views may come to the surface and where disagreement may be acute.

Chapter 33

KEEP STRAIGHT ON TO THE END OF THE ROAD

The song, "Keep straight on to the end of the road", evokes smells, sounds and passions. The mental picture is of soldiers determined to keep fighting and win the war, even if battles are lost along the way. The picture of the soldier conjures up resolve, camaraderie, determination and the ability to overcome pain and hardship.

Sometimes the work environment is unrelenting. There are not enough resources to go round: the pupils are being disruptive and bordering on the anarchic. The customers are being fickle, inconsistent and stroppy. The clients are argumentative, overbearing and irrational. The boss is petulant, unreasonable and indecisive. The staff are slow, thoughtless and disrespectful. The catalogue of woes goes on.

We can feel that the world is against us. Sometimes it is right to be utterly relentless. There are targets that have to be met. There is a product that has to be delivered on time or the financial penalties will be severe. There is a standard that must be maintained for our reputation to be intact. There are deliveries that must be made by the due time. The punctuality rate for the trains has to be above 97% or there are penalties.

The leader or manager sometimes has to be ruthlessly insistent that second best is not acceptable. The resolution to keep straight on to the end of the road may not be a popular strategy in the short term, but sometimes it is absolutely essential, however unpopular it might make the leader.

When a tender proposal has to be submitted by a particular time, there is no alternative, the tender has to be completed. A leader or manager can present a deadline as a powerful motivator, particularly when the consequences of the deadline not being met are made clear. Failure is not an option when it comes to safety on airlines, ships or on major construction projects. Knowing where the line has to be drawn and sticking to that line is part of the responsibility of the manager where the safety of individuals is involved.

Hazel was leading a construction team for a sports stadium. The deadline for completion was fixed well in advance, with sports fixtures already in the diary. There was no scope for slippage. Hazel used this fixed point as the rationale for driving through a project programme with clear obligations on all the contributors. It was relentless, but the impressive look of the new stadium was a powerful incentive for all involved. When some began to suggest it was all too difficult the disapproval of the majority was palpable and the group pressure for compliance was overwhelming.

Sometimes the leader or manager has to appeal to a loyalty and camaraderie that allows unreasonable things to be asked for on a tight timescale. Done with care and tact, demanding requests can produce Herculean responses.

The leader of a voluntary organisation focusing on aid for overseas projects may meet cynicism, apathy and disinterest. The determination to keep advocating the concerns of the charity can feel like pushing a stone uphill. But where the vision is right and there is a clear passion to make a difference, being determined amidst apathy and cynicism may be what is needed. The test for the leader is whether there is enough support and enough belief in what is being done to ensure there is the scope for progress, with cynicism eroded or removed.

HOW DO YOU KEEP STRAIGHT ON TO THE END OF THE ROAD?

- Are you clear about the crucial outcomes?
- How strong is your inner resolve and how can you nurture it?
- What will help keep you focused on the outcomes?
- What is the camaraderie you most need on the journey?
- When might it be right to make unreasonable requests of colleagues?
- What will help you deliver what feels like unreasonable demands?
- How, as a leader or manager, are you both relentless and supportive?
- How do you keep in step with those equally committed to the success of the endeavour?
- How do you test that you are on the right road?

POINTS FOR REFLECTION

- Which of your current activities need dogged resolution?
- How best do you keep up that resolve to reach the necessary outcomes?
- How best do you build a sense of camaraderie with others to keep the resolution and direction that is essential?

Chapter 34

IT IS AN UPSIDE DOWN WORLD

A government director general told me rather sadly that all his champions had now retired or moved on. Those who had supported and backed him were no longer around. He felt alone and at the mercy of politicians and their agendas. This individual did not think he would survive for long. He went on to be a successful permanent secretary and head of his department.

One individual had stayed at a particular grade for many years. Advancement had not come in the way she expected. But all of a sudden she was spotted and promoted and then she moved rapidly up the ladder. The apparent stagnation for a period at one level was unexpected, just as the very rapid promotion was equally unexpected. What made the difference was that she was the right person in the right place at the right time on one occasion, having been out of sight and out of mind on the other. Each decision about promotion had been taken for rational reasons, but the experience of the individual was that these decisions had happened in a haphazard fashion.

Tony Book played non-league football for most of his twenties. He was then spotted by Manchester City and rapidly became established as a first team player and then captain. His was an unexpected and meteoric rise. Equally, a number of footballers play internationally at schoolboy level and then fail to make the grade professionally. Skills can develop in different ways. Happenstance and timing play a major part alongside determination and perseverance.

Accepting that it is an upside down world is necessary for survival. This does not mean accepting unfairness but it does mean being philosophic and recognising that your star can be in the ascendant one day and fall the next. When your star is rising maximise your learning, build your champions, go with the flow and recognise that you are only as good as your last victory. When your star is descending, hold on to what is most important to you, recognise who your real friends are, stick to the values that are paramount and hope for a soft landing.

Sometimes continuity goes out of the window. You have to change or move on. It may mean changing in a way that is against your preferences and even your better judgement. When customers began buying CDs there was no point in continuing to make vinyl records. When young people are willing to go to church only if there are contemporary songs rather than traditional canticles, there is little option but to change what is offered if you want young people to attend.

When the world is turned upside down by economic disaster, there is little point bemoaning the change. If jobs in banking are going, you have to retrain. All we once held dear may be thrown into question when a health scare knocks us sideways. Being diagnosed with Parkinson's disease may mean a radical rethink of our career aspirations. We are thrown into the type of radical reappraisal we had never anticipated. We have no choice: we have to change our aspirations and behaviours.

Gillian was a successful artist, with people travelling many miles to buy her paintings. Unexpectedly, sales began to drop – her style had gone out of fashion and her fans had bought all the pictures they wanted. Did she keep painting the same type of art or did she modify her style? Reluctantly she researched what might sell and began to produce a different type of abstract art. Just as her original market had suddenly collapsed a couple of years before, her new market began to grow. She was thankful her world had been turned upside down.

George was rising fast within the Fire Service. He was sometimes in too much of a hurry, as illustrated by a couple of speeding fines. His bosses had previously viewed him as an energetic, lively young man willing to push the boundaries, but now began to see him as a shade impetuous and irresponsible. His reputation had switched quickly from good to questionable. He knew he had to work on his reputation and rebuild it over time. He was conscious that a good reputation takes time to build, but can be lost quickly.

HANDLING AN UPSIDE DOWN WORLD

- Recognise when the flow is going your way and go with it. When the flow does not go your way, bide your time and build key relationships.
- Do not be too cross and waste emotional energy when others are chosen rather than you. Remember that your time may well come – be ready to take the opportunity.
- Recognise what goes up also comes down.
- Accept the fickleness of fashion.
- Be ready for the unexpected opportunity and seize it with both hands.
- When you feel riled and depressed, try to laugh rather than cry.

POINTS FOR REFLECTION

- In the past, how have you handled what has felt like an upside down world?
- In what ways does your current world feel like being on a rollercoaster, and how best do you hold on to the sides?
- What will help you keep your equilibrium and balance when change is coming at you from many different directions?

Chapter 35

BE WILLING TO TURN SIDEWAYS

Some of the best football managers were not outstanding players. Alex Ferguson, who since 1986 has managed Manchester United, played for various Scottish teams with mixed success. He was in and out of the Glasgow Rangers side. The mix of success and relative failure of some football players gave them a depth of understanding about the game that helped them become outstanding managers. They used their skills and passions in a different role to good effect.

Gus O'Donnell, who was head of the UK Civil Service for six years, talks of a defining moment as an economics lecturer, when his head of department advised him that becoming a top class academic economist might not be a realistic aspiration. This defining moment took him in another direction, working in government as an economist, where he developed an outstanding career. Although fully committed as an economist, Gus had the realism to move sideways into a career that suited him so well.

Bernard was a dedicated public servant who had done a sequence of jobs to outstanding effect, eventually rising to director general level. When two posts were combined, Bernard was not the appointed candidate, but took on a leadership role at a slightly lower level. Bernard never showed any sense of disappointment. He took on this completely different area with energy and commitment. After retiring he moved sideways again and became the chair of a health authority. For Bernard, moving sideways meant fresh opportunities and new ways of bringing his practical good sense and impish humour to bang heads together and move difficult issues to resolution.

When a river reaches big rocks, the water flows around the sides and will always seek to find a new channel. When we find a block in the way we often keep pushing when we would be far better off trying to go round the obstacle. We can learn so many lessons from observing the natural environment, where we see plants growing around rocks or moving sideways to reach sunlight. When you observe nature it can look infinitely adaptable, whereas human nature can often seem irritatingly inflexible.

When I talk with people who feel dejected because of lack of progress in their careers, I invite them to reflect on their generic skills and the extent to which they are useable in other contexts. So often our pride means we want to keep focused on the same aspiration that we have held dear for years, when it is time to modify that aspiration and switch direction. We may be a frustrated head chef, when we could become an excellent teacher. We may be a frustrated academic scientist, when we might be more fulfilled working in industry. We might be a frustrated engineer, when we could enjoy working on development projects in Africa.

Now that careers are much less jobs for life, the question about how to use skills and aspirations to move sideways is pertinent in each decade of our lives. Roger was a solicitor working primarily on divorce cases. He found the work intellectually interesting but emotionally soul destroying. After 20 years he began to hate going to work. But what could he do that would excite him? He had family responsibilities and bills to pay.

Roger chose to put himself forward as a candidate to train for the Anglican ministry. He recognised that, financially, this was a foolhardy move, but he was passionate about enabling people to grow in both their community involvement and in their understanding of faith. He had seen so many broken marriages without hope that he wanted to be in a role where he could nurture faith, hope and love within families. He moved sideways into a different career and six years later he was incumbent in his own parish. He brought the disciplines and rigors of a solicitor into a new world, where he could be passionate rather than clinical. He moved from focusing on marital and human failure into helping bring fulfilment and faithfulness.

WHAT CAN ENABLE YOU TO MOVE SIDEWAYS?

- Try to resist getting too annoyed about obstacles in your way.
- Always look for ways round blockages.
- Be honest with yourself about when you are feeling frustrated and when you are being fulfilled.
- Look at your frustrations through other people's eyes and seek their perspective.
- See moving sideways as an adventure and not as a failure.
- Accept that rekindling your enthusiasm is often best done by moving sideways.
- Be excited about moving into different spheres.
- Be careful that you do not needlessly restrict your choices.

POINTS FOR REFLECTION

- Are you pounding on rocks in your way rather than trying to find a route around them?
- What might happen if you move sideways in your work or in your thinking about aspirations?
- How might you experiment using your generic gifts in a different way, which might open up new, on-going possibilities?

Chapter 36

THREE STEPS FORWARD AND TWO STEPS BACK

Some of the most successful politicians I have worked with have been willing to press their case strongly and then modify their view in the light of comments from others. It might have looked like three steps forward and two steps back, but they have secured one clear step forward. Sometimes, being outrageous in putting forward ideas means that those who oppose you decide not to fight you on every front and you end up making more progress than you had anticipated.

You might be pressing hard for change and believe three steps forward are crucial: then you are disappointed when you are forced into taking two steps backwards. But maybe the time was not right. Other people need time to get used to the idea, and may be more receptive in a year or two. Sometimes progress comes in fits and starts when a new idea becomes more acceptable.

In 1981, when I worked as Principal Private Secretary for Mark Carlisle, the Secretary of State for Education and Science, there was discussion about enabling polytechnics to leave the control of local authorities. When the idea hit the media there was controversy and a campaign to stop this "crazy idea", since it was believed the polytechnics would not be able to survive on their own. The controversy was such that the idea was withdrawn, but seeds had been sown and the desire of the polytechnics for independence grew. A national advisory body was set up and then a separate funding council.

Within 10 years the polytechnics were functioning as independent universities; within 20 years some of the former polytechnics were doing far better than some traditional universities. Although to the polytechnics the withdrawal of the idea in 1981 looked like a backward step, over the next two decades the growth to independence for these institutions was unstoppable. The local authorities that had nurtured the polytechnics needed time to realise that they had to let them go and become independent organisations.

Hannah had a brilliant career in a management consultancy. She had been given a sequence of evermore demanding projects and always seemed to succeed. She had benefited from the patronage of senior people who thought highly of her and was promoted very early to a senior level. But Hannah now had a couple of setbacks: two major projects that she led were relatively unsuccessful. Her star began to wane a little and she became nervous. Hannah felt she did not have the same sureness of touch that she had assumed was always going to be there.

When Hannah took stock she accepted that her reliance on her energy and ability to motivate others needed to be tempered by a more reflective approach about what was possible, as well as developing more subtle ways of working with difficult people. She felt that she needed to take a couple of steps backwards to re-evaluate her approach. But it was well worth doing. She brought a more measured approach that was less based on youthful energy and more on a breadth of experience as she tackled future projects successfully. Hannah accepted that it was right to step back in order to move forward again.

Viewing life as a dance with a sequence of movements, where there are three steps forward and two steps back, can bring a lightness and acceptance that this is the way life is. Experienced dancers flow with the music and move around the dance floor, gliding past other dancers and enjoying the sound and rhythm of the music.

If we engage with our work responsibilities as if it were a dance, we may be going with the flow one moment, and then gliding into a gap in the next, recognising that we have to move backwards and forwards to the dance rhythm. The good dancer uses their footwork to good effect. They avoid bumping into the feet of others by being constantly adaptable, moving back and forth while keeping their balance.

LIVING WITH THREE STEPS FORWARD AND TWO STEPS BACK

- Be curious to see what happens when you take three steps forward.
- Move backwards gracefully, recognising that there will be a net gain.
- See two steps backwards as providing new information and perspectives.
- See life as a dance where movement is continually back and forth.
- Accept that you cannot stand still for too long or you become stiff. Taking a step forward means you see reality from a different perspective.
- Be amused by the movement back and forth.
- Accept that it takes time to generate long-term change.

POINTS FOR REFLECTION

- Where might you press three steps forward?
- How do you currently respond when being pushed back?
- When handling difficult issues, can you imagine your forthcoming movements as if they were part of a dance?
- Where are you stuck where you need to make some steps forward?

PRESENT AND FUTURE

We live in the present but often feel captive to the past and preoccupied by the future. We can spend a lot of time reflecting on the past, asking why we are in the situation we are in. We can be so absorbed with what the future might hold that the present can pass us by. Understanding the past and thinking constructively about the future are both important, but not if the present is squeezed out so that we do not absorb and enjoy what is happening in the here and now.

This section looks at maintaining a balance between the present and the future, while being informed by the past. The intention is to encourage you to link the present and the future together in a way that means you live fully in the present, informed by both the past and the future. The section includes: the future beckons; staying rooted in the past; having one foot in the present and one foot in the future; and letting the future inform the present.

Chapter 37

THE FUTURE BECKONS

Onward and upward. For many years we have believed that each year we will become wealthier, healthier and better informed. Economic improvements, health innovation and information technology developments brought benefits year on year through the latter part of the twentieth century and the early part of the twenty-first century. The future looked ever brighter.

The banking crisis of 2008 and the ensuing recession dampened the assumption that the future is always better. The remarkable developments in health treatment continue but economic change has meant that the future looks more gloomy, with investments and pensions hit hard and the golden years for the baby-boomers looking unlikely to be repeated for future generations.

For the 30 year old in a relatively secure job such as teaching, the future looks OK without being overwhelmingly exciting. For the 40 year old unsure about their job security and seeing their pension fund in decline, the future is uncertain. For the 20 year old with no job and limited employment prospects, the future is bleak. For the 60 year old, healthy retirement may be a new adventure, with both the time and resources to enjoy their "golden years".

When you think of the future, does it excite or depress you? How can we be both ruthlessly realistic about the future while also preparing for opportunities ahead? Feeling positively about the future, and keeping investing in our own personal growth might mean developing skills that are going to be useful now and later. I am forever grateful that I did a post-graduate programme in Executive Coaching when I was aged 55, and completed a doctorate when I was aged 62. There are few things more exciting than seeing someone in their 60s or 70s enjoying a course of learning and equipping themselves to do voluntary work in their communities.

The future may look bleak, but we can influence it. Whatever the external pressures – economic, political or social – upon which we have no influence, we can still make choices. Every day we make choices about our attitude to the future. We are continually making choices about whether we see the future as a land of opportunity or a place of steady decline. Our choice of attitude affects the impact and influence we then have.

In 1995, I was the HR director of a government department that was combined with another department. I was unsuccessful in applying for the role of HR director for the newly-combined department. I readily accepted that the successful candidate was the right appointment for the organisation. I held a party for 200 members of my former department, all of who were unsure about their own futures, as at that point decisions had only been made about board level appointments.

I gave a speech about looking positively to the future, whatever happens to you as an individual. I was speaking from my current experience to many people facing uncertainty. Nearly 20 years later I still get comments from people about the importance of that "wake" and how my speech had helped many facing uncertainty view the future with hope rather than despair.

The challenge is to do hard, realistic thinking about what the future holds while at the same time choosing attitudes and approaches that equip you to handle change and live with the relative degrees of wealth or poverty, and the freedom or limitations, that this brings.

LOOKING TO THE FUTURE

- Be objective about your future financial position.
- Be honest with yourself about your employment prospects.
- Think through any personal development that is worth investing in.
- Recognise the choices that are available to you in terms of both actions and attitudes.
- Observe how others have been influenced successfully in their decisions by their notion of what the future might hold for them.
- Help others to see the future in a constructive way, recognising the spin-off benefit that such conversations might have for you in developing your own thinking.
- Reassess your religious faith and beliefs about human endeavour to see whether they fit into your perspective about the future.

POINTS FOR REFLECTION

- What aspects of the future excite or depress you?
- What opportunities do you have to influence your own future?
- What attitude do you want to have about the decisions you want to make for the future?

Chapter 38
STAYING ROOTED IN THE PAST

When a loved one is elderly and suffering from dementia they can forget the events of the present and remember vividly events of the past. My mother would talk happily about her childhood and her parents. Showing her old photographs would set off pleasures and vivid memories that continue to be cherished. The events of 60 years ago seemed as if they were yesterday. Enabling my mother to celebrate the past was so important to maintaining dignity in the present, which was vague and probably felt meaningless.

The memories we create now will become tomorrow's stories. Enjoying and reliving those stories is not a waste: it means cherishing who we are through the events, circumstances and people that have enabled us to become the person we are.

Our hearts and minds are full of stories of the past, many of which are buried deep in our subconscious. Occasionally, a stimulus reminds us of an event in the past that was very precious at the time but had gone long ago into our subconscious. Sometimes those memories from the past that hit us are joyful moments. Sometimes they are moments of pain, where we regret the actions we took.

Our past has made us who we are. If we ignore our past we may not fully comprehend the mix of influences that have created the distinctiveness within us. But staying rooted in the past and the experiences and values that are most important to us does not mean being captive to the past. The more we understand our own past the more we can be liberated from it and move on.

Understanding the poverty that your grandparents experienced or the sadness they felt through the early death of a child can help explain some of the behaviours of our parents and enable us to be liberated from some of the strictures and attitudes that came down through previous generations.

Understanding the past is just as important in the workings of an organisation. The organisation which understands the influence of past key leaders and knows its heritage may well have a resolve and a character that will enable it to cope with tough times. But if it is too restricted by its heritage, and as a consequence is inflexible in responding to global markets or economic or social change, then the past becomes an impediment rather than something that energises and enables.

Organisations with a religious foundation often bring a heritage and a sense of conviction that motivates their members positively, whatever is happening in the wider world. But that rootedness in the past, as well as being a strength, can lead to conflict, where some members want to respond to the changing social environment and others don't. A church leader wants to both uphold the distinctiveness of marriage and also recognise that living together before marriage is the preferred approach of the majority of couples. The compassionate and realistic priest is able to welcome to the marriage service those who are living together and present an inspiring message about the value and distinctiveness of marriage.

The vegetable that grows well has good roots. It draws moisture from a wide area. It is rooted in soil fertilized with compost formed by decomposed vegetable waste. The vegetable is rooted in the past. The vegetable when harvested becomes food that nourishes, with the vegetable waste beginning the cycle again.

WHAT DOES BEING ROOTED IN THE PAST MEAN?

- Understand the sources of your values and attitudes.
- Understand and be able to retell stories from your family heritage and know how these stories inform your attitude.
- Understand the heritage of organisations of which you are a part.
- Appreciate the people whose memories and characteristics still live on in the organisation.
- Accept when you are stuck in the past and need to move on.
- Recognise how attitudes from the past can inhibit the way an organisation is able to respond flexibly to new opportunities.

POINTS FOR REFLECTION

- In the work you do – or hope to do – what motivates you from your past?
- What from your past inhibits taking forward current opportunities?
- How might you understand aspects of your past more fully?
- What single message of inspiration do you take from your past that is particularly important in looking to the future?

Chapter 39

ONE FOOT IN THE PRESENT, ONE FOOT IN THE FUTURE

We may have memories from our childhood of jumping from rock to rock across a stream when suddenly we slipped and ended up with one foot on a rock and the other in the stream. We feel foolish and elated at the same time! When I was leading a group of walkers on the Dales Way in Yorkshire I began striding across the stepping stones at Bolton Abbey but lost my rhythm and stopped. If I went forwards I thought it likely that one foot would end up in the River Wharfe. To my slight humiliation, and to the amusement of others, I decided that retracing my steps was the safer route. I was teased gently about my failure of courage, but this was not the moment to end up with one foot in the fast-flowing River Wharfe and the other trying to keep a foothold on a stepping stone.

The skier will have experienced two feet wanting to travel in opposite directions, with the result that they are left splayed in the snow. When you run your two feet have to operate in harmony. The long-distance runner needs a rhythm that will use minimum energy over a long period. If one foot begins to falter the runner loses their rhythm and begins to run awkwardly, causing sore hips or strained knees. A high jumper's feet may be doing different things. The jumper will normally launch from the same foot but there has to be a harmony between the action of both feet for the high jumper to be successful.

As the long distance walker goes along the St Cuthbert's Way, there is a point when the front foot may be in England while the rear foot is in Scotland. The feet have to keep moving if the walker is to reach their destination. If you stand for a long time the feet need to be positioned carefully so that the weight can be spread equally for most of the time, even if there might be some movement of weight across the two feet from time to time so the muscles do not tense up.

Having one foot in the present and one foot in the future provides stability and an ability to move forward quickly. The individual who wants to keep a fresh and committed approach is going to be clear about their understanding of the present and receptive about what the future might bring.

The supermarket executive has to ensure that the current needs of customers are met and be mindful of trends so they are responding to changing needs. The best supermarkets recognised that there was a growing demand for gluten free foods and began to highlight the products they offered in this area. By putting one foot in the future they reassured current customers that their changing needs were going to be met.

Frank managed a large farm, and had to ensure that he was maximising his financial return from the crops he was growing, but he also had to keep a careful eye on the future and whether the market price for these products was likely to rise or fall. How much he invested in switching some of his fields from arable to grazing depended on his assessment about future market conditions and the likely action taken by the government. As Frank walked over his fields, deciding which fields to use for the crops that had served him well and which fields to convert to grazing, it was as if he was putting one foot in the present and the other foot in the future.

KEEPING ONE FOOT IN THE PRESENT
AND ONE FOOT IN THE FUTURE

- How much time do you set aside to research future trends?
- How easily do you balance current requirements and future expectations?
- How might you divide your time and resources between doing the tried and trusted well and experimenting with new approaches?
- What are the risks if you do no experimentation?
- How best do you maintain a balance between having one foot in the present and one foot in the future?

POINTS FOR REFLECTION

- How might you balance your focus between the present and the future?
- If you did put one foot more strongly into the future, what would you be doing?
- If you were to plant the other foot more firmly in the present, what would you be doing?

Chapter 40
LETTING THE FUTURE INFORM THE PRESENT

It seems obvious that the past informs the present. We see the legacy of the past all around us. The buildings we observe and the institutions of government, the judiciary, the church and charities are all part of a heritage that lives on in the present. We have no difficulty explaining the links between the past and the present.

We recognise that the present informs the future. Big construction projects will only come to fruition in the future. The investment of time in the education of our children bears full fruit when they become adults. The investment of time, energy and resources in our own personal education and development leads to future fulfilment, satisfaction or advancement.

But we think less often about how the future might influence the present. This might seem like wishful thinking, but reflecting carefully about the future is an essential pre-requisite to living wisely in the present. A government department needs to plan ahead in estimating the likely size of their client groups in the future. The planning of school provision needs to take careful account of demographic trends. Planning health provision needs to be based on rigorous evidence about demographic trends and behaviours.

Bookshops need to respond to the availability of books electronically and the increased move to purchase books online.

They need to take a view about what will continue to draw people into a bookshop. It may be the opportunity to browse in a comfortable environment, or the chance to meet people over coffee, or being close to other points of interest, such as museums, galleries or specialist shops.

Deidre was a clothes' designer. Her reputation could rise or fall quickly, depending on the success of her products. Deidre had to watch trends worldwide – keeping up-to-date with new fashions was crucial. At the same time Deidre had to keep up with changes in technology, so that she understood how complicated patterns could be created efficiently. Deidre kept talking to people in the customer groups she was designing for in order to be conversant with subtle changes in reactions, standards and expectations. Deidre knew that her success depended on keeping an open mind about future trends and to keep listening and learning. There were going to be creations that did not work: she knew she had to live with her failures as well as her successes. But the key criterion was that enough of her new designs were successful to keep her reputation high.

Paul was the director of a business school in a university. He had a good deputy who ran the business school on a day-to-day basis. Paul saw his primary contribution as focusing on the longer term. He invested his time in exploring new markets, such as bringing in international students and developing corporate leadership programmes with major national and international organisations. Paul also had an important role in maintaining the long-term reputation of the university as one that was always looking constructively to the future – hence he wrote an influential paper on the future direction of university-level business education. Paul ensured that the business school kept looking forward and adapting to the market, while ensuring that the current students were well catered for and became good ambassadors for the business school.

HOW BEST DO YOU LET THE FUTURE INFORM THE PRESENT?

- Invest a set amount of resources and time in exploring future trends.
- Create a coherent and compelling view of the future that will motivate people in the present.
- Allow people in your part of the organisation to help create a strategy for the future so that it is owned by everyone and is not just a top-down vision.
- Ensure that trends are plotted forward as accurately as possible, using both firm data and informed assessments.
- Draw on the expertise of those who have a good track record of anticipating future trends accurately.
- Allow yourself to imagine a range of different future options without becoming too tied to one scenario.

POINTS FOR REFLECTION

- Can you set aside some time to anticipate what the future is going to be like?
- How might you use that understanding about the future to influence the way you prioritise your efforts now?
- Who might you talk with about future trends so that current decisions are well informed?

AMBITION AND ACCEPTANCE

Many of us would accept that we have an opportunity to make a difference in our lives. Some of us would say that we have a responsibility to seek to make a positive difference and make the world a better place.

For many there is a strong sense of ambition that comes from personal values and upbringing or the expectations of those around us. Most of us have learnt that acceptance has to sit alongside ambition. We have to balance the desire to make a difference with an acceptance of where it is possible for us to have an impact, and where it would be foolhardy to believe that transformation on the scale we would like is possible.

In this section we look at whether being single-minded is good or bad; when acceptance is a sign of strength rather than weakness; the determination to know when you can make a difference and when you cannot; and the progress that can come through both ambition and acceptance.

Chapter 41

BEING SINGLE-MINDED: GOOD OR BAD?

My younger son was single-minded in wanting to excel at playing ultimate frisbee. He played for Surrey University when he was a 17-year-old schoolboy, captained the GB Under 19 team and the Bristol University team, and also represented Great Britain in the World Championships. He was single-minded in pursuit of his ambition. However, by the age of 24 he was beginning to accept that other aspects of life were going to squeeze the amount of time he could give to playing the sport at international level. He accepted there were limits to his ambition.

A newly-appointed vicar may be single-minded in devoting themselves to the work of the parish but they can become too single-minded for their own good if all their efforts and energy goes into work. The new vicar, in order to thrive over a long period, needs to ensure that he or she takes days off and has protected family time. They need to do physical exercise for their health as well as have friendships and intellectual interests outside work.

"All work and no play makes Jack a dull boy" is true in any sphere. Too much ambition and the life is sucked out of an individual. They cease to be of value to people outside work and their family life can become strained and lacklustre.

The ability to be single-minded is a great strength. William Wilberforce was single-minded in his desire to abolish the slave trade. He was, in his own words, "diligent in the business of life" in his focus on pursuing reform. Behind most health, education and social changes have been champions who have devoted their energy to the delivery of radical change. Scientists have been single-minded in their quest for breakthroughs that have taken health innovation to places never previously expected. Our lives have been hugely improved because health scientists have had an unrelenting ambition to solve medical dilemmas.

As a customer we want shops, garages, railways, public transport and the insurance industry to be single-minded in providing us with the best possible service. We are never satisfied and demand even more. Through the way we make decisions as consumers we are fuelling the requirement that organisations demand single-minded ambition from their staff, so that the quality of products and services is ever higher. We do not want to accept lower quality services: we will take our custom elsewhere if we are not satisfied.

Decisions by customers create the positive effect of forcing service providers to be single-minded in keeping quality high. But the service provider may well be using this pressure to grind out from their suppliers the last drop of effort at the lowest possible price. As individuals, sometimes we might choose to accept a slightly lower quality of service because we are getting work done by local suppliers or by those providing work for young offenders as part of their rehabilitation. Sometimes our ambition to help people in our community or locality might mean consciously accepting a lower quality of service.

Henry was single-minded in his work in the finance department in producing the best quality management accounts. But his single-mindedness could turn into abrasiveness. Some individuals in the company were reluctant to share information with him and his task became more and more difficult. He needed to be just as single-minded about the end product, but modify his approach. A desire to be single-minded in winning people over needed to sit alongside a focus on ensuring the best possible accounts.

WHEN IS BEING SINGLE-MINDED APPROPRIATE?

- Is the task and the timetable agreed?
- Has the purpose of what you are doing been effectively communicated?
- How best do you win doubters over to the importance of what you are doing?
- How best do you test whether your single-mindedness is right in a particular situation?
- Who will give you feedback as to whether your approach is working effectively?
- How will you ensure your single-mindedness at work does not detract from the open-mindedness that is important in the rest of your life?

POINTS FOR REFLECTION

- When you are being single-minded, how do you ensure you do not become too blinkered?
- How do you keep an awareness of when your single-mindedness can be counter-productive in other areas of your life?
- What situations are coming up soon where you need to be single-minded?

Chapter 42
ACCEPTANCE AS A SIGN OF STRENGTH AND NOT WEAKNESS

Acceptance is often viewed as weakness, but can be a sign of great strength. Accepting our physical limitations means that we pace ourselves and begin to use our energy in a more focused way. Accepting our intellectual limitations means that we cease trying to win every argument and focus our energies on what is most important to us.

Acceptance involves self-awareness. Self-knowledge is an important starting point: we need to understand our abilities, preferences, limitations and idiosyncrasies. If we understand ourselves well we are less likely to put ourselves into situations where we let ourselves down. When we understand how we work best we are much more likely to accept working jointly with others who have complementary skills and experience.

If any team is going to work well there has to be an acceptance of the strengths and weaknesses of each of its members. The boss who expects each team member to be perfect is going to be disappointed. The good boss knows his people, appreciates their strengths and recognises their less strong areas. The boss will want to bring a strong sense of ambition and energy, but in a way that accepts and enjoys colleagues as they are.

The manager has no choice but to take account of their boss's guidance, as the boss has authority and responsibility. The individual working for the boss cannot ignore that authority: they have to live with it. But acceptance does not mean blind acquiescence. Acceptance of the role of the boss still means that the individual can influence and persuade their boss – but there is little point in pretending that the boss has no authority or power.

The dilemma is: what do you accept and what do you try and change? Sometimes, the timing is not right and a situation has to be accepted as it is. On other occasions it is right to push for radical change and be persistent and determined in that intent.

Ray worked for a consultancy that ran major IT projects. He believed that success resulted from contractual arrangements – which included a clear sharing of risk – but his current bosses did not favour this approach. He decided to bide his time, to continue developing his thinking and approach, to test it out with different experts and to have it ready at the right moment. When the organisation's current approach began to falter he was as helpful as possible in suggesting modifications.

In one reflective stock-take session Ray judged the timing was right to mention an alternative approach. His ideas were listened to, so he suggested that he work with two or three others to develop them further. He gradually built a group of four people who helped shaped the new approach. The organisation readily switched to this new approach. In retrospect, he judged that his timing had been right. He needed to accept the reality of the views of his boss and choose his timing carefully. His success came from waiting rather than being dogmatic.

Age can affect both our physical and intellectual capacities. Pacing ourselves becomes essential. It forces us to be more selective about the use of our time and energy. Accepting when we can make the most useful contribution is a sign of both age and maturity.

ACCEPTANCE CAN BE A SIGN OF STRENGTH AND NOT WEAKNESS WHEN:

- Others have legitimate authority and responsibility.
- Your allies are few in number and you would lose the vote.
- The moment is not yet right.
- Expressing your concerns might be counter-productive, because it will enable others to embed existing stances.
- You are better off focusing your energies on other things.
- The benefits do not outweigh the investment cost.
- Acceptance is consistent with you maintaining your integrity and the values that are most important to you.

POINTS FOR REFLECTION

- When in the past has acceptance been a strength or a weakness?
- When has a period of acceptance enabled you to build your case for change at a later date?
- When has acceptance meant that you have been able to use your energy and focus in an effective way?
- What are you accepting now that you should not accept?
- What are you accepting now where you know your acceptance is about biding your time for a new opportunity?
- Where might you want to say, "I am going to accept this situation no longer?"

Chapter 43

KNOWING WHEN YOU CAN MAKE A DIFFERENCE AND WHEN YOU CANNOT

Shortly after I became Regional Director for the UK Government in the North East of England in 1991 there were riots in Meadowell and West Newcastle. In a relatively traditional part of the country with a high regard for law and authority, these riots were a rude awakening. The rioters focussed their destruction on their own communities, which had few stable families, high levels of unemployment and lack of trust in the police and authorities.

As a consequence there was a shared resolve among politicians, public servants, business leaders and the voluntary sector to try to make a difference. There was investment in housing and new jobs, a radically different policing policy, practical support for community leaders and the physical environment was improved. Educational standards showed some progress. Relations with the police were now based on a more secure foundation of trust. However, dysfunctional families continued to be disruptive and gang aggression remained just below the surface. Car crime and drugs were still problems.

Was this shared effort through City Challenge and other approaches a success or failure? There were lots of positive changes because of the determination to make a difference by a wide range of different people. But the action was only partially successful in dealing with some families and individuals, who remained persistently resistant. The lesson from this and many other similar initiatives is that people in communities only change when they decide they want to. The "doing good" intentions of those from outside may be a catalyst and enabler, but individuals and communities must have that desire to solve their own problems for change to happen successfully and be sustained.

When a rugby team has a winger in their three-quarter line who is a superb defender, the opposition that focuses its attack on this player's side of the field is unlikely to be successful. The adept three-quarter line will focus their attack on the other side of the field. The good sports coach will have looked carefully at the strengths of the opposition and will be coaching the players to focus their efforts on where they can make a difference rather than where the opposition is particularly strong.

In large companies a skilful influencer will understand the strengths and foibles of key people in the organisation. They will know whose backing they need in order to win a particular argument. They will know who has fixed views and will be difficult to persuade. The key judgements are: who do you influence in a gentle way, who do you have to tackle "head on", and who can you sideline or ignore? It can seem manipulative, but this is the reality of life in politics and big organisations.

Adapting your approach to meet the requirements of a situation and the key individuals in that situation is a necessary skill. Working with many government ministers over 32 years taught me that each minister needed to be treated in a different way. I got it right with many and spectacularly wrong with a couple. With one of them it was patently clear I was never going to build the right relationship and so it was time for me to move on. With another a faltering initial relationship turned into a strong bond.

Sometimes we are determined to make a difference in the way we approach issues. It is right that we seek to become more confident, experienced and adaptable in our approach, but we are who we are and cannot change our basic character. We will always have personal preferences, however much we adapt and grow our repertoire of approaches. A good level of self-knowledge includes understanding when we can adapt our approach and reactions, and when it is not realistic to significantly change our approach and we simply have to live with who we are.

KNOWING WHEN YOU CAN MAKE A DIFFERENCE AND WHEN YOU CANNOT

- What evidence do you have from past situations that can help you decide when it is possible to make a difference?
- What does your intuition tell you about what is possible or not possible?
- How much energy and time are you willing to invest to make a difference in this situation?
- How will you react if you fail to make a difference?
- How wide a mix of influencing and persuading approaches are you willing to embrace?
- At what point will enough be enough?

POINTS FOR REFLECTION

- What have you learned from past situations where you have been able to make a difference in some areas and not in others?
- What have you learned about yourself, the types of approach you used and the types of situations that can be changed or are resistant to change?
- Looking forward, can you reflect on a complicated situation where you would like to make a difference? How will you decide on your approach while accepting that you are unlikely to be completely successful?

Chapter 44

PROGRESS THROUGH BOTH AMBITION AND ACCEPTANCE

The word "ambition" often gets a bad press. It can imply self-centredness and ruthless single-mindedness. Ambition can appear destructive to personal values and family life but without ambition, the world would be in a sorry state. Ambition has led to major improvements in education, healthcare, quality of life and the services we enjoy. We want the chief executive of a charity to be ambitious in raising funds and pushing the boundaries of what is possible. We want the vice chancellor of a university to be ambitious in building the best possible institution in which students can learn.

Ambition is important for many people. The ambition to keep learning keeps our minds active. It can be instructive to reflect on where our ambition comes from and how we handle it. I suspect mine came from being an only child in a single parent family, following my father's death when I was aged seven. My mother was determined that I should do well at school. As a Christian there was a strong sense of ambition to make a difference for good in both the work and community contexts. Sometimes, my ambition had to be reined in. After being interviewed, unsuccessfully, on two separate occasions for the post of university vice chancellor, I had to recognise that this route was never going to open for me as I did not have the necessary academic credentials.

Progress comes through acceptance as well as ambition. Winston Churchill had to live with a relative degree of failure in a number of different ministerial posts, but this did not dampen his resolve to lead Britain against fascism. As a wartime prime minister, he brought all the strength of focused ambition and experience from what had worked less well in the past.

We have no option but to accept our character, our parents, our cultural background and our personal history. We can feel hard done by or resentful about elements of our heritage, but that can make us twisted and drain our energy and resolve. Accepting who we are and how we are made, rather than fighting against it, can provide us with the stability to be ambitious and build from our strengths and characteristics. We have been dealt a particular set of cards and it is for us to decide how to use them. Being aggrieved that we have been dealt the wrong set of cards is a waste of energy.

Judith enjoyed being a head of department at a comprehensive school. Her ambition was to be a head teacher and she felt a strong sense of vocation for this type of role. Judith felt she had the right approach and perspective: colleagues believed in her. Judith began to build up expertise that would equip her for senior posts. She went on all the necessary training courses and progressed to a deputy head post with relative ease.

But did she really want to become a head teacher? She hesitated about taking on the ultimate responsibility. Would she want to be on call in an emergency, 24 hours a day? Would she want the public criticism if examination results were not good? How would she handle school inspections that were critical? Judith knew that she would have to accept a degree of pressure and inroads into her personal life that were more than she wanted.

Judith was unsuccessful in a couple of applications for head teacher posts and accepted that she was not going to be an automatic first choice. For Judith, acceptance was about being patient and finding a post that matched her qualities. When

Judith was finally appointed to a headship she reflected on the importance of her ambition and her acceptance of her own strengths and weaknesses.

PROGRESS THROUGH BOTH AMBITION AND ACCEPTANCE

- Do you fully understand the sources of your ambition?
- Are you willing to see your ambition as a good thing or are you suspicious of it?
- How can you use your ambition in a positive and constructive way?
- How readily can you accept your limitations?
- How do you accept decisions that do not go your way constructively?
- How often has acceptance enabled you to progress through recognising that some doors have been closed?
- How easily do you reconcile ambition and acceptance as you review what has happened to you over the last year?

POINTS FOR REFLECTION

- Think about an ambition you have: what are your next steps in taking it forward?
- Think about something you are resisting that you need to accept.
- How best do you balance your ambition to make a difference with an acceptance of what is or isn't possible?

SERIOUS AND JOYFUL

A graduation ceremony can be both serious and joyful. A memorial service for someone who has died after living a full life can also be both serious and joyful. But in a disaster or crisis there is no room for joy. There are also times when there should be unalloyed joy, with no hint of seriousness to dampen the spirits.

Life is an oscillation between being serious and joyful. In a single day, we may be switching from a focus on joy and encouragement to the delivery or receipt of a serious message. One of the secrets of a successful and happy life is the capacity to balance the serious and the joyful, and know how to move through different situations, combining a deep appreciation of the serious with a joyful and light heart.

This section looks at living life with a purpose, seeing the bigger picture, laughing at yourself and asking, where do I fit in?

Chapter 45

LIVING LIFE WITH A PURPOSE

It is a delight sometimes to wander aimless as a cloud. There are times when we want to be going with the wind and be shaped by the currents around us. Being pushed by winds from different directions can be invigorating.

Part of recuperating after a busy period is letting go and allowing our thoughts to go where they will. Lying out in the sun with our eyes closed can be a time when we empty our minds, drift in our thoughts and become revived by the fresh air and the sun.

If we spent all day drifting with the wind or being baked by the sun, we would either disappear into oblivion or be baked to a cinder. After resting a while we want to get up and get on. There are things to be done, there are decisions that need to be taken. There are relationships that need to be nurtured. There are plans that need to be made. There are conversations that need to be had.

We can, and should, stop and stand for a while. The space we gain when we stand and stare gives us perspective and allows the unconscious to process thoughts and feelings and crystallize what is important. When the processing has been done we can feel a greater sense of what are the right next steps. Sometimes it is about tentative steps, on other occasions we have a new clarity of direction.

Living life with a purpose is rarely about delivering just one overriding priority. Living life with a purpose is about balancing different intentions: being a good colleague, a competent manager, a supportive parent, a thoughtful spouse or partner and a responsible member of the community. We may be living with a variety of different priorities, with our wellbeing depending on the inter-connectedness between those priorities and their relative equilibrium. In some moments the dominant priority may be our family and on other occasions it may be our community or work. Balancing our priorities requires agility and constant re-evaluation of what is more or less important.

But underlying this mix of priorities is likely to be a central purpose, or purposes, that provide the hard drive for our actions. Our central purpose may come from our religious beliefs, our personal philosophy, our cultural background or our family values. For many of us, the purpose that is most important reflects all these strands. Being clear about our purpose is not about fulfilling trite aspirations: it is rooted in what is important to us and where we want to make a difference.

As we reflect on our purpose, we might bring together an understanding of our gifts, a sensitivity to the needs of those around us, a recognition of the opportunities that are before us and an awareness of what is at the core of our personal philosophy or beliefs.

Beryl felt pushed around and insignificant in the bank where she worked. No one seemed to take her seriously. She did not seem to be able to make any difference to the attitudes around her or make a useful contribution. She felt dispirited. She was looking for a new sense of purpose.

Beryl enjoyed her evenings as a Brownie leader. She loved encouraging children to learn and grow. She felt she had no purpose at work and a rich purpose at the Brownies. Beryl decided to train as a teacher. It was a bold step with a reduction in income. But Beryl had a strong sense of purpose that she could be an effective teacher. The training was tough, the first year had its ups and downs, but by the third year Beryl loved teaching. She had found her sense of purpose. There was an underlying joy in all she did as a teacher.

LIVING LIFE WITH A PURPOSE

- What purpose would take forward your family heritage and values?
- What sorts of purposes fire your imagination?
- In what areas of your life do you feel the greatest sense of fulfilment and personal contribution?
- What blind alleys have you been down that have given you insight into what isn't purposeful to you?
- What type of legacy do you want to leave behind that reflects the sense of purpose you want to develop?
- What sense of purpose might be deep within you?
- What sense of purpose might seem trite but is worth exploring?
- With whom can you share your most personal thoughts about the purpose, or purposes, that are growing within you?

POINTS FOR REFLECTION

- What type of future purpose most excites you?
- How might you explore such ideas further?
- What would be the effect of taking forward with more deliberate intent the current purposes that are important to you?

Chapter 46
SEEING THE BIGGER PICTURE

In January 2012 the Royal Academy hosted an exhibition by the artist David Hockney entitled, "A Bigger Picture". David Hockney has in recent years painted large vistas on inter-connected canvasses, which take the viewer deeply into the landscape. The exhibition included a remarkable set of four vast paintings entitled *Three Trees near Thixendale, Winter 2007*, which portrayed the winter, spring, summer and autumn. Not only are the pictures vast, but they are set in a wide landscape and show the changing seasons with colour, charm and clarity.

David Hockney's pictures bring out the colour and vitality in the most straightforward of views. In my home, we have on a wall a print of a barley field painted by David Hockney, with its bright colour and texture bringing radiance and life. As you look at the picture you are engaged by the simplicity and excitement of what you see. David Hockney paints a bigger picture and brings you into a scene full of colour and energy.

Getting the balance right can be about being on the dance floor and the balcony at the same time. It is about being involved enough to see what might need to be done at a micro level. But it is also having the desire and the capacity to stand back and observe, and see the bigger picture.

Seeing the bigger picture is about being alert to what is going on at more than one level. It is seeing the emotional dynamics as well as the interplay of the arguments. It is sensing what really matters to people in terms of ultimate purpose rather than practical short-term gain. It is appreciating the link between short-term priorities and long-term outcomes. Seeing the bigger picture is often about dreaming dreams of what might be possible. It is thinking beyond the normal pattern of expectation to create a future that is more than just a replication of the past.

Seeing the bigger picture involves creating the stepping stones that will get us to that destination. When you walk through foothills in the Scottish mountains and look up to see the peak you want to climb, it stands proud as part of a landscape that inspires you. Then it is one step in front of another, one ridge climbed with another coming into view, as one stretch of the walk is completed and further phases are tackled.

Seeing the bigger picture is holding together in our minds the destination we want to reach, the conditions that will help or hinder our progress, the colleagues who will help or hinder us and the practical milestones we need to reach to get to our destination in reasonable time.

John was a highly accomplished accountant working in a medium-sized company. He was appreciated for what he did, but he knew he had to look at the bigger picture. He needed to take a view about whether he wanted to stay in accountancy or move into general management. Did he want to stay as a specialist in a smaller company or move to a bigger organisation where there might be more opportunities? He needed to think through whether his company was going to thrive or grow, or whether the economic conditions meant he was better moving elsewhere.

John recognised that while his colleagues appreciated his contribution this did not mean that his future was guaranteed. He needed to think about the big picture issues for himself and take responsibility for his own decisions. He had to weigh up what might happen to his company and his profession alongside his own personal circumstances.

John decided that he had to take time to talk to friends, one or two trusted colleagues and a coach. He thought hard about what was most important for him and what elements of the bigger picture were clear and which were constantly evolving. John decided to move to a bigger organisation and put more emphasis on his professional development. Others in similar situations may have reached different conclusions, but John knew that his focus on the bigger picture had helped him work through important, practical issues.

SEEING THE BIGGER PICTURE

- Move backwards or sideways to observe your current situation from a different perspective.
- Ask yourself, what is the bigger picture? Write down your answers.
- Try to project yourself into the future in your current role to see the potential opportunities and pitfalls.
- Visit an art gallery and see whether studying a painting can help you piece together your current situation in a different way.
- Go to a high viewing point and look at the vista ahead. See how different components fit into the overall landscape, and use that as an analogy for your own situation.

POINTS FOR REFLECTION

- Can you see some of the issues you are dealing with as part of a bigger picture?
- Imagine those issues as a small part of a bigger canvas. See whether your current positioning on the canvas feels light or dark.
- Reflect on what would need to happen for you to move into a lighter space.

Chapter 47

LAUGHING AT YOURSELF

What happens when you look in the mirror? Do you see a wise and generous-hearted person or do you see a tired and weary individual who is not really you at all? Unfortunately, the mirror rarely lies. We are as the mirror captures us, whether we like it or not.

Perhaps surprisingly, if you laugh at yourself in the mirror, your image laughs back at you. If you scowl at yourself, you get a scowl back. The mirror has a remarkable ability to play back to us the demeanour or emotion we are exhibiting to others.

Our world is more full of mirrors than perhaps we realise. When we smile at someone, their natural reaction is to smile back. When we scowl at someone else, their instinctive reaction is to reflect our scowl. If we are feeling bright and cheerful, or low and beleaguered, a similar reaction can come back at us from those around us.

In my Civil Service career I observed many earnest individuals and groups trying to impress the Secretary of State of the day about the rightness of whatever they happened to advocate. The intensity of some of the representations could feel like a powerful rolling wave. The only way to combat such intensity was to put up a thick, strong and high wall. The result was big, crashing waves and little progress. The waves just hit the brick wall and bounced back.

Those who had more impact on successive Secretaries of State were those who put their arguments clearly but also brought a lightness of touch. They came with a desire to build a rapport and a shared understanding. They represented their case with warmth and understanding, without diluting the importance of their arguments. When they brought a light touch and some humour into the room, they were far more likely to be listened to. The Secretary of State was more likely to be disarmed and open as a result of genuine interest and concern.

Laughing at yourself is about recognising your own foibles and idiosyncrasies. It is about seeing the funny side in any situation and recognising that you do not get it right all the time. Something that goes wrong should not be seen as a doom-laden act of failure but as something to learn from and perhaps even joke about.

When we laugh at ourselves, we are more likely to be able to adjust our behaviour in the future. If we take ourselves too seriously, we can become cross with ourselves, beat ourselves up and get stuck in a spiral of feeling inadequate.

Laughing at ourselves is infectious. If we can be amused by our own idiosyncrasies and can recognize the ridiculous in any situation, then others are more likely to relax and be more ready to learn from their own experience.

Janette was small, slight and softly spoken. Most of her colleagues were large men who physically looked down on her. Janette was tough and liked to be seen to be tough. These men felt a bit humiliated by her sharp tone of voice. They were reluctant to come and see her and would never share any of their concerns or willingly seek her advice.

Janette recognised that she needed to change her approach. She began to smile more. She made jokes about her relative small size. She was more complimentary about what her colleagues were doing. Janette began to make her colleagues laugh. They knew that inside this more light-hearted exterior there remained an iron hand in a velvet glove, but they began to loosen up a bit too, and now felt less apprehensive about talking through their concerns with Janette. Showing that she could laugh at herself changed her relationship with her colleagues, who now saw her more as an ally than a threat.

HOW MIGHT YOU LAUGH AT YOURSELF MORE?

- Look for the ridiculous, laugh at it and share the joke.
- Share stories about when you have missed the point.
- Allow the inner chuckle to show.
- Keep smiling even though everyone else is scowling.
- Recognise when there is a twinkle in someone's eye and acknowledge it.
- Drop by to talk with people who lighten your spirits.
- Talk about things in the work environment that have made you laugh.
- When you are tempted to take yourself too seriously, don't.

POINTS FOR REFLECTION

- Can you imagine work situations you will be in over the next few days where you can bring a lighter touch and enable others to smile?
- Can you see the ridiculous and build a shared sense of humour?
- When might you laugh at yourself and allow that to show?

Chapter 48
WHERE DO I FIT IN?

Am I a round peg in a round hole, or a square peg in a round hole? Am I fitting in too comfortably and, therefore, happy with inaction? Or do I not fit in well and feel uncomfortable, unappreciated and irrelevant? Perhaps the ideal is to fit in well enough so that you are trusted, appreciated and listened to, but not so well that you feel inactive, complacent and uncreative.

There is a human need to be accepted and fit in. We want our working relationships to be harmonious and constructive. We want to contribute to outcomes that matter. Therefore, some creative dialogue and thoughtful argument is central to our success and wellbeing.

We want to create a coming together of different ideas which sparks new energy. We do not want friction that debilitates. A sense of shared endeavour needs to be dynamic and creative, where there is a place for me and my contribution. I want to be part of a group or team that is making a difference. I fit in because I am making things happen.

I am a piece of the jigsaw which, when linked with other pieces, creates a bigger picture and a clarity of vision. I do not mind about the shape of my jigsaw piece provided it can fit with others and together create a bigger picture that is attractive, that stimulates thought and action, and brings a smile to people's faces. Fitting in well starts from recognising your strengths, interests and contribution. It is then about listening to others and where they come from and what their issues are. It is blending your contribution into the bigger picture. It is folding your words within the wider dialogue. It is recognising and embracing the emotional dynamics within the organisation. It is coming back to the central purpose: why you are there in the first place, what is the contribution you want to make, and what outcome you want to see delivered.

Sometimes you might sense that you do not fit in and it is time to move on. Expectations might have changed, the skill base might be different, and the market has evolved. You may feel disappointed or even resentful that you do not fit in as before. But life and organisations are dynamic. You may not be changing as rapidly as the organisation. Where there was once a smooth join, there can now be a rough edge. When we fit no more it is time to be honest with ourselves, recognise the changing reality and be willing to move on with a sense of expectation about the new and not resentfulness about what has passed.

Asking the question, "Where do I fit in?" can take us into new areas and new thoughts. Do you need to move to a different part of the organisation or to a new organisation? Would it be helpful to view work and the rest of your life in a rather different way? Are there other types of hopes and aspirations it would be good to pursue? Perhaps the existing jigsaw has become a bit stale and repetitive. You need to see if there is another jigsaw into which you can fit.

Rarely will there be a perfect fit. If the fit was perfect there would be no room for manoeuvre and you would be stuck. Perhaps you need a bit of space to wriggle and experiment. Perhaps your jigsaw is changing continually and, therefore, the space in which you are best suited may have altered compared to a few years ago.

Can you enjoy the dynamic nature of life and work even more? As technology, markets, attitudes and customer expectations change, can you celebrate the changes and not be too wary of them? You may not be sure how well you will fit into the changing jigsaw in the future but if your frame of mind is that you want to keep learning, listening and watching, then you are likely to be adaptable and enjoy future changes rather than be inhibited by them and resentful of them.

WHERE DO I FIT IN?

- Is the shape of my jigsaw piece changing?
- What sort of jigsaw would I like to be a part of in the future?
- Are the rough edges of my jigsaw piece helpful or a cause of irritation?
- How do I want my jigsaw piece to change its shape in the future?
- How many jigsaws do I want to be part of at the same time?
- How ready am I to celebrate the whole picture of the jigsaw rather than just the section in which I fit?

POINTS FOR REFLECTION

- Can you see where you are a good fit and where you are a less good fit?
- How important is that fit to you?
- How can you make a good fit work well to ensure progress is made?
- When the fit is less good, how can the rough edges or gaps provide the space for finding a creative way forward?

ACKNOWLEDGEMENTS

Over the last nine years I have had the privilege of working with many individuals and groups as they have wrestled with getting the balance right. The conversations have often been journeys of discovery, where individuals have addressed their own values, beliefs, hopes and demons. I have gained so much in my own understanding through a wealth of conversations. I have sought to distil this understanding into this book, which I hope will be a valuable source of ideas for those who read it.

I am grateful to Jeremy Oates, with whom I have had many insightful conversations on the themes in this book. I am grateful to him for agreeing to write the foreword to this book.

Jackie Tookey has been a superb typist in turning my words into elegant prose. Helen Burtenshaw has been immensely valuable in organising the different sections of the manuscript into a complete whole.

I am grateful to Paul Gray and Hilary Douglas who, as colleagues at Praesta Partners, have helped me maintain a clear focus at a practical level on what getting the balance right means.

I am indebted to the patience of Frances, my wife, as I have put this book together. Through her wise words, she helps me find balance in my life much better than I would otherwise have done.

I have dedicated this book to Anna, Owen and Holly, who have become much cherished members of our family as the spouses, respectively, of our children Graham, Ruth and Colin.

OTHER BOOKS BY PETER SHAW

- *Mirroring Jesus as Leader.* Cambridge: Grove, 2004.
- *Conversation Matters: how to engage effectively with one another.* London: Continuum, 2005.
- *Finding Your Future: the second time around.* London: Darton, Longman and Todd, 2006.
- *The Four Vs of Leadership: vision, values, value-added, and vitality.* Chichester: Capstone, 2006.
- *Business Coaching: achieving practical results through effective engagement.* Chichester: Capstone, 2007 (co-authored with Robin Linnecar).
- *Making Difficult Decisions: how to be decisive and get the business done.* Chichester: Capstone, 2008.
- *Riding the Rapids: how to navigate through turbulent times.* London: Praesta, 2008 (co-authored with Jane Stephens).
- *Deciding Well: a Christian perspective on making decisions as a leader.* Vancouver: Regent College Publishing, 2009.
- *Raise Your Game: how to succeed at work.* Chichester: Capstone, 2009.
- *Defining Moments: navigating through business and organisational life.* Basingstoke: Palgrave/Macmillan, 2010.
- *Effective Christian Leadership in the Global Workplace.* Colorado Springs: Authentic/Paternoster, 2010.
- *Seizing the Future.* London: Praesta, 2010 (co-authored with Robin Hindle-Fisher).
- *Living Leadership: finding equilibrium.* London: Praesta, 2011.
- *The Reflective Leader: standing still to move forward.* Norwich: Canterbury Press, 2011 (co-authored with Alan Smith).
- *Thriving in Your Work.* London: Marshall Cavendish, 2011.
- *The Age of Agility.* London: Praesta, 2012 (co-authored with Steve Wigzell).

FORTHCOMING BOOKS

- *Leading Through Demanding Times.* Cambridge: Grove, 2013 (co-authored with Graham Shaw).
- *The Emerging Leader.* Norwich: Canterbury Press, 2013 (co-authored with Colin Shaw).
- *100 Great Personal Impact Ideas.* London: Marshall Cavendish, 2013.
- *Celebrating Your Senses.* London: SPCK, 2013.
- *Effective Leadership Teams: a Christian perspective.* London: Darton, Longman and Todd, 2014 (co-authored with Judy Hirst).
- *Sustaining Leadership.* Norwich: Canterbury Press, 2014.

ABOUT THE AUTHOR

Peter Shaw works with individuals, teams and groups to help them grow their strengths and tackle demanding issues confidently. His objective is to help individuals clarify who they want to be, the values that drive them, the value-added they want to bring to their work and their sources of vitality. His work on how leaders step up successfully into demanding leadership roles and sustain that success has recently been recognised with the award of a Doctorate by Publication from Chester University.

Peter's clients enjoy frank, challenging conversations leading to fresh thinking and new insights. It is the dynamic nature of the conversations that provide a stimulus for creative reflection and new action. He often works with chief executives and board members taking on new roles and leading major organisational change. Peter has worked with chief executives and senior leaders in a range of different sectors and countries. He has led workshops across five continents with themes such as "Riding the Rapids", "Seizing the Future", "Thriving in your Work" and "Building Resilience".

Peter has held a wide range of board posts covering finance, personnel, policy, communications and delivery. He has worked in five UK Government departments (Treasury, Education, Employment, Environment and Transport). He delivered major national changes, including radically different pay arrangements for teachers, a huge expansion in nursery education and employment initiatives that helped bring unemployment below a million.

He led the work on the merger of the UK Government departments of Education and Employment. As Finance Director he managed a £40bn budget and introduced radical changes in funding and accountability arrangements. In three director general posts he led strategic development and implementation in major policy areas.

Peter has written a sequence of influential leadership books. He is a Visiting Professor at the University of Chester and a Visiting Professor of Leadership Development at Newcastle University Business School. He has worked with senior staff at the University of Brighton and with postgraduate students at the Warwick Business School and at Regent College in Vancouver, Canada. He was awarded a CB by the Queen in 2000 for his contribution to public service.

Peter is a Reader (licensed lay minister) in the Anglican Church and has worked with senior church leaders in the UK and North America. His inspiration comes from long distance walking: he has completed eleven long distances walks in the UK, including the St Cuthbert's Way, the South Downs Way, the Yorkshire Wolds, the Yorkshire Dales Way and the Great Glen Way.